HOLLYWOOD TALENT AGENCY DIRECTORY

Title: Hollywood Talent Agency Directory

ISBN-13: 978-1-942825-28-9

Author: Kambiz Mostofizadeh

Publisher: Mikazuki Publishing House

Copyright: 2020. All Rights Reserved.

Description: Directory of Hollywood Talent Agencies used for Actors, Actresses, Production companies, Casting Agents, and Directors.

HOLLYWOOD TALENT
AGENCY DIRECTORY

Rae Model & Talent Agency LLC
414 Mason Street, Suite 705
San Francisco CA 94102

James Weissenbach dba Weissenbach
Management
5951 Airdrome Street
Los Angeles CA 90035

Paradigm Talent Agency LLC
8942 Wilshire Boulevard
Beverly Hills CA 90211

Shinn Entertainment Corporation dba
International
191 E. City Place Dr.
Santa Ana CA 92705

Ford Models, Inc.
11 E. 26th St., Floor 14
New York NY 10010

Closeup Models, LLC
5455 Wilshire Blvd, Suite 2020
Los Angeles CA 90036

Craig Scagnetti dba Jack Scagnetti Agency
5136 Vineland Ave
North Hollywood CA 91601

DGReps Inc.

HOLLYWOOD TALENT AGENCY DIRECTORY

7083 Hollywood Blvd.
Los Angeles CA 90028

I0102133

David Michael Hewitt
Enterpri 638 Lindero Canyon Rd #240
Oak Park CA 91377

Phillip L. Brock dba Studio Talent Group
1328 12th Street
Santa Monica CA 90401

Willow Model Management LLC
206 W. 4th Street #425
Santa Ana CA 92701

Prestige Talent Agency, Inc.
9100 Wilshire Blvd., Ste. 725E
Beverly Hills CA 90212

Deborah Graci dba Talents Hunters
23216 Respit Dr
Lake Forest CA 92630

John E. Hutcheson dba BOOM! MODELS AND TALENT
2339 3rd Street, #49
San Francisco CA 94107

Crown North Talent Management Inc.

HOLLYWOOD TALENT
AGENCY DIRECTORY

1045 North El Dorado St., #12
Stockton CA 95202
John T. Paizis dba 98 West Talent
231 E. Spruce Ave.
Inglewood CA 90301

Carrie Macy dba Carrie Macy Talent Agency
9595 Wilshire Blvd. Ste. 900
Beverly Hills CA 90212

DPM Talent Agency, Inc.
14520 Magnolia, #202
Sherman Oaks CA 91403
No Ties Management, LLC
434 West Cedar Street, Suite 200
San Diego CA 92101

Bonnie Howard dba Howard Talent West
17000 Ventura Blvd
Encino CA 91316

Media Artists Group Inc.
8222 Melrose Ave, Suite 203
Los Angeles CA 90046

The Polygon Group, Inc.
303 N Glenoaks Blvd., Suite 200
Burbank CA 91502

HOLLYWOOD TALENT
AGENCY DIRECTORY

Metric Models LLC
628 1/2 Sunset Ave
Venice CA 90291

Green and Green Talent Group
6363 Wilshire Blvd., Ste 420
Los Angeles CA 90048

M.O.B. INC.
6404 WILSHIRE BLVD #505
LOS ANGELES CA 90048

VINCENT ANTHONY CESARANI dba THIRD
WAVE ASSOCIATE
6320 CANOGA AVENUE SUITE 1502
WOODLAND HILLS CA 91367

EPIC ENTERTAINMENT, LLC
77570 SPRINGFIELD LANE STE J
PALM DESERT CA 92211

RUSSELL TODD dba RUSSELL TODD
AGENCY
5238 GOODLAND AVENUE
VALLEY VILLAGE CA 91607

JORDAN LEE, INC. dba GOLD LEVIN TALENT
8424A SANTA MONICA BLVD #706
LOS ANGELES CA 90069

HOLLYWOOD TALENT
AGENCY DIRECTORY

THE SAVAGE AGENCY, INC.
1041 N. Formosa Ave. E. Bldg. Ste 103
West Hollywood CA 90046

It model management, LLC
5151 California Ave. #100
Irvine CA 92617

Kyle Scudiere dba Influence Artist Agency
1600 Main Street
Venice CA 90291

MARTIN HALLEN & DANIELA M. WULFF dba
PTI Talent
1710 N. MOORPARK RD., # 215
THOUSAND OAKS CA 91360

LIAISON ARTISTS LLC
2343 3RD STREET. SUITE 299
SAN FRANCISCO CA 94107

Closeup Models and Talent, LLC
5455 Wilshire Blvd., Suite 2020
Los Angeles CA 90036

PATTY A. MEZIN & EDWARD N. GOLDBERG
dba Chic Mode
5150 E. Pacific Coast Hwy., Suite 200
Long Beach CA 90804

HOLLYWOOD TALENT
AGENCY DIRECTORY

Beverly J. Graham dba THE BEVERLY
AGENCY
2337 Roscomare Rd.
Bel Air   CA 90077

Willow Model Management, LLC
26341 Jefferson Avenue, #F
Murrieta CA 92562

Littman Talent Group, Inc.
4500 Park Granada, Suite 202
Calabasas CA 91302

Maven Artists Agency LLC
269 South Beverly Drive #204
Beverly Hills CA 90212

Cox Modeling LLC
9900 Stirling Road, Suite 226
Cooper City FL 33024

Tack Artist Group, LLC
7288 W. Sunset Blvd., #207
Los Angeles CA 90046

WORLD MODELING TALE
9619 Canoga Avenue
Chatsworth CA 91311

HOLLYWOOD TALENT
AGENCY DIRECTORY

JEP Entertainment Group, Inc.
2083 Booth Street
Simi Valley CA 93065

Kingvigor Inc.
4522 Woodman Ave C312
Sherman Oaks CA 91423

Monterrey Artist Inc. dba Monterrey
Productions
3737 Stockdale Hwy, Suite 220
Bakersfield CA 93309

International Talent Agency LLC
9701 Wilshire Blvd., Suite 1000
Beverly Hills CA 90212
Tiffany Richer dba RPM Talent
2600 W. Olive Ave., 5th Floor
BurbankCA 91505

City Model Management, Inc.
500 3rd Street, #580
San Francisco CA 94107

Cadenza Artists LLC
1000 Granville Avenue, Suite 301
Los Angeles CA 90049

Pantheon Talent Group, LLC dba Pantheon

HOLLYWOOD TALENT
AGENCY DIRECTORY

1801 Century Park East #1910
Los Angeles CA 90067

AB2 Talent, LLC
11601 Wilshire Boulevard, Ste 500, 5th Floor
Los Angeles CA 90025

All Access Talent, Inc.
121 W Lexington Dr Ste 414
Glendale CA 91203

Filmtrix, Inc. dba THE FILMTRIX AGENCY
5124 COLDWATER CANYON AVE, #209
SHERMAN OAKS CA 91423

Lovestone Talent Agency, LLC
7772 Santa Monica Blvd.
West Hollywood CA 90046
Hollywood Original Talent
6115 Selma Avenue, Suite 207
Los Angeles CA 90028

Trio Talent Agency
1502 N. Gardner St.
Los Angeles CA 90046

Tracey Mattingly, LLC
717 N. Highland Ave., #9
Los Angeles CA 90038

HOLLYWOOD TALENT
AGENCY DIRECTORY

Luke Johnstone dba Dig-It Talent
77 Shotwell Street, Unit 3
San Francisco CA 94103

Villatoro Research LLC dba Villatoro Talent
8160 Manitoba St. #115
Playa Del Rey CA 90293

Lita D. Schloss aka Leigh Castle dba Castle Hill
1101 South Orlando Ave.
Los Angeles CA 90035

The Irv Schechter Company
9460 Wilshire Boulevard, Suite 300
Beverly Hills CA 90212

SUMMIT TALENT
9454 Wilshire Blvd., Ste. 203
Beverly Hills CA 90212

Luminary Talent
550 South Hill Street, Suite 1607/A262
Los Angeles CA 90013

Arcadio M. Castillo
4115 GLENCOE AVE. #114
MARINA DEL REY CA 90292

HOLLYWOOD TALENT
AGENCY DIRECTORY

Nancy Chaidez Agency & Associates, Inc.
6340 Coldwater Canyon Avenue Unit 214
North Hollywood CA 91606

NYX Models
809 San Miguel Avenue
Venice CA 90291

NMG Management Group, Inc. dba Napoli
Management
8844 West Olympic Blvd Suite 100
Beverly Hills CA 90211

Sarah Yapelli dba Black Apple Talent
1112 Montana Ave Unit 609
Santa Monica CA 90403

Palomera De La Ree Producciones dba
PALOMERA GROUP
1460 NW 107 Ave Suite Q
Miami FL 33172

Steven Cutler dba Catalyst Talent Agency
12424 Wilshire Blvd, 9th Floor
Los Angeles CA 90025

PlushTalent Modeling Agency
10844 Modena Terrace
Philadelphia PA 19154

HOLLYWOOD TALENT
AGENCY DIRECTORY

Dizon Artist Agency
560 Mission Street Suite 1300
San Francisco CA 94105
Career Artists International
11030 Ventura Blvd. #3
Studio City CA 91604

Todd Cote dba Leafy Green
2180 Bryant Street Suite 206
San Francisco CA 94110

Next Management LLC
15 Watts Street
New York NY 10013

Marc Chancer
4705 Laurel Canyon Blvd. #203
Valley Village CA 91607

Nu Talent Agency, Inc.
117 North Robertson Blvd Suite A
Los Angeles CA 90048

Scott Stuart Reifman dba Odds On Agency
802 North Vista Street
Los Angeles CA 90046
Susanna Griffith Talent
155 North Lake Avenue Suite 800

HOLLYWOOD TALENT
AGENCY DIRECTORY

Pasadena CA 91101

Chances Unlimited
12400 Wilshire Blvd Suite 850
Los Angeles CA 90025

Michael R. Voelkel dba Golden Stars Talent
1424 4TH STREE, #228
Santa Monica CA 90401

Global Talent Agency LLC
2615 West Magnolia Blvd Suite 101
Burbank CA 91505
Innovative Productions, Inc.
2525 16th Street, # 304
San Francisco CA 94103

The Mirisch Agency
8840 Wilshire Blvd Suite 100
Beverly Hills CA 90211

Rage Models
23586 Calabasas Road Unit 104
Calabasas CA 91302

High Road Touring LLC
751 Bridgeway Third Floor
Sausalito CA 94965

HOLLYWOOD TALENT
AGENCY DIRECTORY

Lenhoff Enterprises Incorporated
100 S. Doheny Drive, #214
Los Angeles CA 90048

Paradise Artists, Inc.
108 East Matilija Street
Ojai CA 93023

The Ross Agency, Inc.
5150 East Pacific Coast Highway Suite 200
Long Beach CA 90804

Fred R. Price Talent Agency
14044 Ventura Blvd. Ste. 201
Sherman Oaks CA 91423

Avalon Artists Group Inc
5455 Wilshire Blvd, Suite 900
Los Angeles CA 90036

Limelight Talent Inc
8149 Santa Monica Blvd Unit 287
Los Angeles CA 90046

Tonry Talent
885 Bryant Street Unit 201
San Francisco CA 94103

HOLLYWOOD TALENT
AGENCY DIRECTORY

Lewis & Beal Talent Agency
3406 W. Burbank Blvd
Burbank CA 91505

BMG Models
5455 Wilshire Blvd Suite 900
Los Angeles CA 90036

David Shapira and Associates Inc.
193 N. Robertson Blvd
Beverly Hills CA 90211

Power Talent Agency, Inc.
2305 Historic Decatur Rd
San Diego CA 92106

AP Robertson Taylor Agency LLC
11500 West Olympic Blvd Suite 400
Los Angeles CA 90064

Bell Hall Talent, Inc dba BH Talent
16430 Ventura Blvd suite 200
Encino   CA 91436

THE STEIN AGENCY, INC.
5125 Oakdale Ave
Woodland Hills CA 91364

HOLLYWOOD TALENT
AGENCY DIRECTORY

Daniel Swan dba Swan Entertainment
2600 Tenth Street Suite 433
Berkeley CA 94710

EEM Law, PC
13932 Emelita St.
Valley Glen CA 91401

Progressive Artists Agency Corp
9696 Culver Blvd, Suite 110
Culver City CA 90232

310 Artists Agency
3500 West Olive Avenue Unit 300
Burbank CA 91505

Michael Beltran
2665 Ariane Drive #207
San Diego CA 92117

Kathleen Schultz Associates
6442 Coldwater Canyon Suite 206
Valley Glen CA 91606

AMK Hollywood Talent Agency
2223 West Colorado Blvd
Los Angeles CA 90041

HOLLYWOOD TALENT
AGENCY DIRECTORY

T3 Talent
464 E Main St Suite 4
Spartanburg SC 29302

Affinity Models and Talent, Inc
5455 Wilshire Blvd Suite 1010
Los Angeles CA 90036

Greg Scuderi and Oscar Arce
15315 Magnolia Blvd Suite 430
Sherman Oaks CA 91403

The Janet Williamson Music
2120 Roselin Place
Los Angeles CA 90039

O'Neill Talent Group, LLC
4150 Riverside Drive Suite 212
Burbank CA 91505

Sandra Marsh & Associates
6420 Wilshire Blvd., Ste. 880
Los Angeles CA 90048-5538

25 Live, LLC
25 Music Square West
Nashville TN 37203

HOLLYWOOD TALENT
AGENCY DIRECTORY

Cynthia Booth dba Singular Talent
9358 W. Olympic Blvd
Beverly Hills CA 90212

Cameron Talent & Modeling Agency, LLC
2500 Broadway, Building F, Suite#F-125
Santa Monica CA 90404

Farallon Entertainment LLC
538 Duncan Street
San Francisco CA 94131

Almond Talent Agency
8217 Beverly Blvd Suite 8
Los Angeles CA 90048

The Jerry Pace Agency
8383 Wilshire Blvd, Ste 800
Beverly Hills CA 90211

Event Model Group LLC
7080 Hollywood Blvd Suite 1100
Los Angeles CA 90028

Richard Luna
2518 1/2 Main Street
Santa Monica CA 90405

HOLLYWOOD TALENT
AGENCY DIRECTORY

Michael Pick International Inc
12100 Wilshire Blvd Suite 1030
Los Angeles CA 90025

Commercial Talent Inc
12711 Ventura Blvd Suite 285
Studio City CA 91604

Jennifer Renee Colquitt
4605 Sylmar Avenue Suite 306
Sherman Oaks CA 91423

Cynthia Young Barry
13440 Ventura Blvd Suite 211
Sherman Oaks CA 91423

The Talent House LA
3770 Highland Ave. Suite 201
Manhattan Beach CA 90266

Stephen Leung dba So Cal Talent
16882 Bolsa Chica St., Ste 108
Huntington Beach CA 92649

SCORE A SCORE, LLC
8455 Beverly Blvd ste 309
Los Angeles CA 90048

HOLLYWOOD TALENT
AGENCY DIRECTORY

Condra Artista Talent Agency
2600 West Olive Ave. 5th Floor
Burbank CA 91505

Theresa Worhach dba WILD BRIAR TALENT
2620 W. Main St.
Alhambra CA 91801

Common Chord, LLC
25 Madison Avenue
New York NY 10010-8601

Daniel Fiamingo dba StatusSilver
2468 Claremont Pl
Union City CA 94587

The Crofoot Group, Inc.
4123 Park Verdi
Calabasas CA 91302

Schneider Entertainment
22287 Mulholland Hwy Suite 210
Calabasas CA 91302

Envy Model & Talent LLC
489 S. Robertson Blvd., #104A
Beverly Hills CA 90211

HOLLYWOOD TALENT
AGENCY DIRECTORY

Greene and Associates Talent Agency
1901 Avenue of the Stars, STE 130
Los Angeles CA 90067

Digital Development Management, Inc.
17 New South St., Suite 205
Northampton MA 01060

Career Artists International
11030 Ventura Blvd., #3
Studio City CA 91320

Susan Nathe and Associates Commercial
Performer's
9903 Santa Monica Blvd.
Beverly Hills CA 90212

INSURGE-ENT, LLC
2144 North Junipero Avenue
Palm Springs CA 92262
Bella Agency LLC
6430 Sunset Boulevard, Suite 460
Los Angeles CA 90028

John Pierce Agency Inc
3270 Casitas Ave.
Los Angeles CA 90039

HOLLYWOOD TALENT
AGENCY DIRECTORY

Aqua LLC
9000 Sunset Blvd Suite 700
West Hollywood CA 90009

Bell Talent Inc
40992 Calle Pueblo
Indio CA 92203

Croce Talent
6215 Monterey Rd
Los Angeles CA 90042

Third Hill Entertainment, Inc.
195 South Beverly Drive Suite 400
Beverly Hills CA 90212

Innovative Artists Broadcast Division LLC
1505 Tenth Street
Santa Monica CA 90401

Connor Ankrum and Associates Inc
1680 North Vine Street Suite 916
Los Angeles CA 90028

Screen Artists Agency LLC
16505 Arminta Street
Van Nuys CA 91406

HOLLYWOOD TALENT
AGENCY DIRECTORY

Fast Solutions Inc dba BETWIXT TALENT
1110 Rose Avenue
Venice CA 90291

Frank Elliot Shapiro Talent Agency, LLC
5522 Lemona Avenue
Sherman Oaks CA 91411

Wrenn Management LLC
7805 Sunset Blvd. #211
Los Angeles CA 90046

Bienstock LLC dba Bienstock
888 7th Avenue, Suite 913
New York NY 10106

TGMA LLC
1645 North Vine Street PH 1002
Los Angeles CA 90028

Firestarter Entertainment LLC
4304 Wildwest Circle
Moorpark CA 93021

Yuliya Rodriguez dba JVC Talent Agency
11030 Ventura Blvd Suite 2
Studio City CA 91604

HOLLYWOOD TALENT
AGENCY DIRECTORY

MMV LLC
4221 Wilshire Blvd Suite 290-3
Los Angeles CA 90010

Stars, The Agency
23 Grant Avenue 4th Floor
San Francisco CA 94108

Midwest Talent Management Inc
11211 Cohasset Street
Sun Valley CA 91352

Paula McAfee dba Starcraft Talent Agency
27525 Newhall Ranch Road Suite 7D 2nd Floor
Valencia CA 91355

Eagle Eye Agency LLC
8600 Burton Way Unit 301
Los Angeles CA 90048

Culinary Artists Agency Inc
13017 Woodbridge Street
Studio City CA 91604

Ken Lindner and Associates Inc
2029 Century Park East Suite 1000
Los Angeles CA 90067

HOLLYWOOD TALENT
AGENCY DIRECTORY

ValMaur Talent Agency
6671 Sunset Blvd Bldg 1585 Suite 108
Hollywood CA 90028

AC Talent Agency LLC
8447 Wilshire Blvd PH
Beverly Hills CA 90211

Stewart Talent Management LA, Inc
1601 Vine St., 6th Floor
Los Angeles CA 90028

Factor Model Management LA Inc
7250 Melrose Avenue Suite 4
Los Angeles CA 90046

Kim Lee Osgood dba Zephyr Talent Agency
418 Bamboo Lane, Ste.A
Los Angeles CA 90012

Janet Elizabeth Rosenberg
1140 Prospect Heights
Santa Cruz CA 95065

Donna Lee Farrow & Teddy Jacobs dba
Blacktie Ente
13603 Marina Pointe Drive Unit D331
Marina Del Rey CA 90292

HOLLYWOOD TALENT
AGENCY DIRECTORY

Imperium7, LLC
5455 Wilshire Blvd Suite 1706
Los Angeles CA 90036

Smith & Hervey / Grimes Talent Agency LLC
3002 Midvale Avenue Suite 206
Los Angeles CA 90034

Deborah DeOliveira / Lea Anne Wolfe
811 N Ontario St.
Burbank CA 91505

Mavrick Artists Agency Inc
8447 Wilshire Blvd, Suite 301
Beverly Hills CA 90211

David Belenzon Management Inc.
2067 First Avenue
San Diego CA 92101

Brady, Brannon & Rich, LLC
5670 Wilshire Blvd Suite 820
Los Angeles CA 90036

Model Agency Acquisition, Inc.
11500 W. Olympic Blvd., Suite 400
Los Angeles CA 90064

HOLLYWOOD TALENT
AGENCY DIRECTORY

Prima Eastwest Model Mgmt
8618 West Third Street
Los Angeles CA 90068

Lloyd D Robinson
136 El Camino Drive Suite 410
Beverly Hills CA 90212

2020 Inc.
468 N. Camden Dr., Suite 200
Beverly Hills CA 90210

Charlotte Gusay
10532 Blythe Avenue
Los Angeles CA 90064

Stars Model Management
23 Grant Avenue 4th Floor
San Francisco CA 94108

William Kerwin Agency
1605 North Cahuenga Blvd Suite 202
Hollywood CA 90028

AKA Talent Agency
4525 Wilshire Boulevard, Suite 280
Los Angeles CA 90010

HOLLYWOOD TALENT
AGENCY DIRECTORY

Maria Matias Music, Inc.
28182 Robinson Canyon Road
Carmel CA 93923

Aruni Sasasmith Blount
717 Pine Avenue
Long Beach CA 90813

Angelika Schubert, Inc. dba Celestine
7250 Melrose Avenue, Suite 6
Los Angeles CA 90046

Exclusive Artists Mgmt, Inc.
7700 West Sunset Blvd Suite 205
Los Angeles CA 90046

Magdalena Talent, Inc.
1600 Rosecrans Ave
Manhattan Beach CA 90266

DeRossi Ellis and Hubbard Network Media
117 E Colorado Blvd Suite 600
Pasadena CA 91105

L.A. Models, Inc.
7700 Sunset Blvd
Los Angeles CA 90046

HOLLYWOOD TALENT
AGENCY DIRECTORY

Reign Agency, LLC
400 South Beverly Drive Suite 250
Beverly Hills CA 90212

Del Entertainment, Inc.
6400 Garfield Ave
Bell Gardens CA 90201

Z Entertainment Group
4721 Laurel Canyon Boulevard
Valley Village CA 91607

The Brogan Agency LLC
1517 Park Row Venice CA 90291

Commercials Unlimited, Inc.
10300 Wilshire Blvd.
Los Angeles CA 90024

Sean Cawley dba CAWLEYWOOD
304 Holly St.
Laguna Beach CA 92651

Hussie Models, LLC
8939 Sepulveda Blvd Suite 102
Los Angeles CA 90045

HOLLYWOOD TALENT
AGENCY DIRECTORY

Phillip L. Hawkins dba Pittmobile Talent Agency
1800 Vine Street, #334
Hollywood CA 90028

Cactus Creatives Los Angeles, LLC
1436 North Martel Ave, #212
Los Angeles CA 90046

William Morris Endeavor Entertainment, LLC
9601 Wilshire Blvd., 3rd Floor
Beverly Hills CA 90210

Linda McAlister Talent LLC
4218 Santa Monica Boulevard
Los Angeles CA 90029

Wunder International, LLC
332 S Beverly Dr
Beverly Hills CA 90212

360 Models LLC
7106 Owensmouth Ave (Rear Unit)
Canoga Park CA 91303

Wasserman Media Group, LLC
10900 Wilshire Blvd. Suite 1200
Los Angeles CA 90024

HOLLYWOOD TALENT
AGENCY DIRECTORY

Jason Lee Record
8283 1/4 B Santa Monica Blvd
West Hollywood CA 90046

Scott & Ann Inc,
6100 Wilshire Blvd Suite 1500
Los Angeles CA 90048

OSCAR P. GRANT dba MLH LITERARY AND
TALENT AGENCY
8939 S. Sepulveda Blvd., Ste 110-142
Los Angeles CA 90045

Krengel Spamer Vance LLC dba Domain
1880 Century Park East, Suite 1100
Los Angeles CA 90069

JACK LIPPMAN AGENCY, INC.
9151 SUNSET BLVD
WEST HOLLYWOOD CA 90069

Siona Entertainment
14724 VENTURA BLVD PH
SHERMAN OAKS CA 91403

FORTRESS TALENT MANAGEMENT, INC.
23901 CALABASAS ROAD, SUITE 2016
CALABASAS CA 91302

HOLLYWOOD TALENT
AGENCY DIRECTORY

LIBERTALIA ENTERTAINMENT, LLC
18627 BROOKHURST STREET #396
FOUNTAIN VALLEY CA 92708

Jacqueline Michelle Sale dba S5 Talent
8484 Wilshire Blvd, Ste 515
Beverly Hills CA 91316

DIVA CENTRAL TALENT AGENCY
7190 W. Sunset Boulevard, #1445
LOS ANGELES CA 90046

Amsel, Eisenstadt & Frazier A Talent & Literary
5055 Wilshire Blvd., #865
Los Angeles CA 90036

Mannequin Models
7912 Northlake Dr #105
Huntington Beach CA 92647

Tiffany Ann Gonzalez dba Connected Actors
Agency
7371 Fountain Ave Apt 304
Los Angeles CA 90046

Paloma Model & Talent, Inc.
1600 Rosecrans Avenue, Media Center, 4th
Floor

HOLLYWOOD TALENT
AGENCY DIRECTORY

Manhattan Beach CA 90266

David Thomas Style
10866 Wilshire Blvd, Ste. 650
Los Angeles CA 90024

BRUSHED, INC.
690 E. LADERA STREET
PASADENA CA 91104

THE BLACKWELL FILES, LLC.
3178 17TH STREET UNIT 3
SAN FRANCISCO CA 94110

MARY KATHARINE MAYER dba ANGEL CITY
TALENT
8318 KIRKWOOD DRIVE
LOS ANGELES CA 90046

COLLIDE AGENCY, LLC
5514 WILSHIRE BLVD FL 9
LOS ANGELES CA 90036

MARGARET ROIPHE AKA MAGGIE ROIPHE
dba MAGGIE ROIP
1721 SOUTH GARTH AVENUE
LOS ANGELES CA 90035

Christina Price dba Worldwide Artists Group
1999 Avenue of the Stars Suite #1100
Los Angeles CA 90067

HOLLYWOOD TALENT
AGENCY DIRECTORY

CUNNINGHAM, ESCOTT, DIPENE AND
ASSOCIATES, INC. d
10635 SANTA MONICA BLVD #130
LOS ANGELES CA 90025

BARBARA ANN RUNGE dba Vibe
Entertainment
338 WESTBROOK PLACE
COSTA MESA CA 92626

LOOK MODEL AGENCY
333 Bryant St Suite 370
SAN FRANCISCO CA 94107

KEEP PRODUCTIONS, INC.
4605 LANKERSHIM BLVD, STE 200
NORTH HOLLYWOOD CA 91602

MCDONALD-SELZNICK ASSOCIATES, INC.
3575 Cahuenga Boulevard, #390
Los Angeles CA 90068

LA SIERRA PROMOTIONS INC.
8628 VAN NUYS BLVD
PANORAMA CITY CA 91402

JANE RACHAEL SCHULMAN dba VESTA
TALENT AGENCY
1600 ROSECRANS AVENUE, 7th Floor
MANHATTAN BEACH CA 90266

HOLLYWOOD TALENT
AGENCY DIRECTORY

ROBERT EATMAN ENTERPRISES, INC.
917 Corsica Drive
Pacific Palisades CA 90272

SOLID TALENT, INC.
22222 SHERMAN WAY, STE. 102
CANOGA PARK CA 91303

ROCKET SCIENCE TALENT, INC.
4500 PARK GRANADA BLVD., STE. 202
CALABASAS CA 91302

GENESIS ARTISTS AGENCY
8383 WILSHIRE BLVD SUITE 345
BEVERLY HILLS CA 90211

L. A. TALENT, INC.
7700 W. SUNSET BLVD
LOS ANGELES CA 90046

IEG Impression Entertainment Group dba IEG
IMPRES
555 W. 5th Street, 35th Floor
Los Angeles CA 90013

PRODUCTION FIT MODELS LLC 830
TRACTION AVENUE, SUITE 3A
LOS ANGELES CA 90013

HOLLYWOOD TALENT
AGENCY DIRECTORY

PACIFIC TALENT & MODELS, INC.
1600 ROSECRANS AVENUE 4TH FLOOR
MANHATTAN BEACH CA 90266

Atlas Talent Agency/LA, Inc.
15 East 32nd Street, 6th Floor
New York NY 10016

David M. Patton Talent Agency
10065 E. Becker Lane
Scottsdale AZ 85260

Mother Jones, LLC
7119 W. Sunset Blvd. Ste. 203
Los Angeles CA 90046

Ring Monkey Promotions dba Avail Talent
14608 Whitter Blvd.
Whittier CA 90605

ENTERTAINMENT AMERICA AGENCY INC.
1093 HIGHLAND PARK
FALLBROOK CA 92028

DEBORAH ANN VIENA dba MOXIE MODEL
AND TALENT
111 W. OCEAN BLVD SUITE 400
LONG BEACH CA 90802

HOLLYWOOD TALENT
AGENCY DIRECTORY

THE EMPIRE AGENCY, INC.
30077 AGOURA COURT SUITE 230
AGOURA HILLS CA 91301

YOUTH TALENT CONNECTION, INC.
17332 IRVINE BLVD #230
TUSTIN CA 92780

MJB TALENT AGENCY LLC
7449 MELROSE AVENUE SUITE #6
LOS ANGELES CA 90046

KAREN RENNA dba KAREN RENNA &
ASSOCIATES
1320 RUBERTA AVENUE
GLENDALE CA 91201

MCHUGO ARTISTS AGENCY, LTD.
6912 Owensmouth Avenue, Suite 101
Canoga Park CA 91303

SPECIAL ARTISTS AGENCY, INC.
9200 SUNSET BLVD STE 1170
WEST HOLLYWOOD CA 90069

THE BEDDINGFIELD COMPANY, INC.
13600 VENTURA BLVD #B
SHERMAN OAKS CA 91423

HOLLYWOOD TALENT
AGENCY DIRECTORY

COAST TO COAST TALENT GROUP, INC.
3350 BARHAM BLVD
LOS ANGELES CA 90068

Organic Talent, LLC
1016 Wilcox Ave., Ste. 9
Los Angeles CA 90038

JAIME FERRAR
4370 Tujunga Avenue, Suite 335
Studio City CA 91604

GRACE MARIAN CHAN dba GRACE MODEL
MANAGEMENT
12400 Ventura Blvd., #421
Studio City CA 91604

WILD MODELS, INCORPORATED
269 S. BEVERLY DRIVE #217
BEVERLY HILLS CA 90212

CENTRAL ARTISTS INC.
1023 North Hollywood Way, #102
BURBANK CA 91505

DONALD LYLE FRANKEN & ANDREW
LAWRENCE WOOLF
5777 W. CENTURY BLVD, #1070
LOS ANGELES CA 90045

HOLLYWOOD TALENT
AGENCY DIRECTORY

Metropolitan Talent Agency, Inc.
6121 Sunset Boulevard
Los Angeles CA 90028

THE MINE AGENCY
6121 Sunset Blvd.
LOS ANGELES CA 90028

MOMENTUM TALENT & LITERARY AGENCY,
3500 WEST OLIVE AVENUE, SUITE 300
BURBANK CA 91505

DATTNER DISPOTO AND ASSOCIATES
304 S. BROADWAY, SUITE 405
LOS ANGELES CA 90013

#1 TALENT AGENCY, INC.
555 W. 5th Street, 34th Floor
LOS ANGELES CA 90013

CINDY ROMANO MODELING AND TALENT
AGENCY, INC.
73-101 HIGHWAY 111 SUITE #7
PALM DESERT CA 92260

ARTISTRY dba SHELDON PROSNIT
AGENCY, LYONS SHELDO
800 S. ROBERTSON BLVD, SUITE 6
LOS ANGELES CA 90035

HOLLYWOOD TALENT
AGENCY DIRECTORY

Socialebs, LLC
3900 San Fernando RD, Suite 1013
Glendale CA 91204

Sherman Davis, Jr., Consulting and
Management Group
433 N. Camden Drive #400
Beverly Hills CA 90210

THE GORFAINE/SCHWARTZ AGENCY, INC.
4111 W. ALAMEDA AVENUE #509
BURBANK CA 91505

DTA AGENCY, LLC dba DT MODEL
MANAGEMENT
883 Westbourne Drive
West Hollywood CA 90069

LEMON LIME AGENCY, INC.
3245 Casitas Ave., Suite 107
LOS ANGELES CA 90039

BOPPIE BOODAH, INC. dba The Corsa
Agency
11849 West Olympic Blvd., #100
LOS ANGELES CA 90064

HOLLYWOOD TALENT
AGENCY DIRECTORY

ABRAMS ARTISTS AGENCY, INC.
750 N. SAN VICENTE BLVD, TOWER 11TH
FLOOR
LOS ANGELES CA 90069

DARREN JAY LEWIS
17328 VENTURA BLVD #428
ENCINO CA 91316

The MDME Agency, LLC
7080 Hollywood Blvd. #1100
Los Angeles CA 90028

RAYMOND A. CAVALERI dba CAVALERI &
ASSOCIATES TAL
3500 W. OLIVE AVE SUITE 300
BURBANK CA 91505

ALLEGORY CREATIVE TALENT, LLC
13261 MOORPARK STREET, SUITE 103
SHERMAN OAKS CA 91423

VICKI ROBERTS AND ARTHUR ANDELSON
dba KISMET TALE
3435 OCEAN PARK BLVD, SUITE 107
SANTA MONICA CA 90405

HOLLYWOOD TALENT
AGENCY DIRECTORY

M MODEL MANAGEMENT, LLC dba M
MODEL MANAGEMENT
8113 MELROSE AVENUE #3
LOS ANGELES CA 90046

ALYCIA R. STARK dba STARK TALENT
12777 West Jefferson Boulevard, Bldg D, Suite
300
Los Angeles CA 90066

FLICK EAST-WEST TALENTS, INC.
9057 NEMO STREET
WEST HOLLYWOOD CA 90069

Luciano Reeves Talent, Inc.
21700 Oxnard St., Suite 950
Woodland Hills CA 91367

LYN BALDWIN dba BALDWIN TALENT
AGENCY
8055 W. MANCHESTER AVENUE #230
PLAYA DEL REY CA 90293

ANNETTE VAN DUREN dba Annette Van
Duren Agency
3810 WILSHIRE BLVD #1906
LOS ANGELES CA 90010

HOLLYWOOD TALENT
AGENCY DIRECTORY

CAST IMAGES MODEL & TALENT AGENCY,
2530 J STREET STE 203
SACRAMENTO CA 95816

MARTA DAVIS dba HOLLYWOOD -
VANCOUVER-NEW YORK TAL
1010 WILSHIRE BLVD SUITE 910
LOS ANGELES CA 90017

KATE WARD dba THE WARD AGENCY
1617 N. EL CENTRO AVENUE - SUITE 25
HOLLYWOOD CA 90028

AMATRUDA BENSON & ASSOCIATES, INC.
433 N. CAMDEN DRIVE SUITE 400
BEVERLY HILLS CA 90210

JKA TALENT & LITERARY AGENCY, INC.
8033 SUNSET BLVD. SUITE 915
LOS ANGELES CA 90046

JIM LENNY & KIM LANG dba JACK LENNY
ASSOCIATES
9454 WILSHIRE BLVD SUITE 600
BEVERLY HILLS CA 90212
TANYA BRANNON dba JKL Talent
444 WEST OCEAN BLVD., STE. 800

HOLLYWOOD TALENT
AGENCY DIRECTORY

LONG BEACH CA 90802

CRAIG ALLEN JONES dba FILM THEATRE
ACTORS EXCHANGE
390 28TH AVENUE #3
SAN FRANCISCO CA 94121
CONCRETE BOOKING AGENCY, ltd.
141 Halstead ave Suite 4
Mamaroneck NY 10543

David J. Freedman & Jack Gaw
5255 Veronica St.
Los Angeles CA 90008

PROST MARKETING, INC.
130 STANFORD DRIVE
SAN ANTONIO TX 78212

Salt Model & Talent Agency, LLC
11500 Olympic Blvd., Ste. 400
Los Angeles CA 90064

NOEL JONATHAN PALM dba ELEMENT
TALENT AGENCY
201 N. Brand Blvd. suite 200
Glendale CA 91203

HOLLYWOOD TALENT
AGENCY DIRECTORY

ROTHMAN/ANDRES ENTERTAINMENT, LLC
4400 COLDWATER CANYON AVENUE #235
STUDIO CITY CA 91604

KRAFT-ENGEL MANAGEMENT LLC
15233 VENTURA BLVD SUITE 200
SHERMAN OAKS CA 91403

SHAMON FREITAS & COMPANY, INC.
3916 OREGON STREET
SAN DIEGO CA 92104

JOSEPH LE TALENT AGENCY
3500 WEST OLIVE AVENUE #300
BURBANK CA 91505

GVA TALENT AGENCY, INC.
193 N. ROBERTSON BLVD.
BEVERLY HILLS CA 90211

Eleven Talent Agency, Inc.
121 West Lexington, Suite 258
Glendale CA 91203

KL GROUP, INC. dba SOCIETY 15
9623 CANOGA AVENUE
CHATSWORTH CA 91311

HOLLYWOOD TALENT
AGENCY DIRECTORY

CASSELL-LEVY, INC.
6032 WILKINSON AVENUE
NORTH HOLLYWOOD CA 91606

TCA JED ROOT, INC.
9220 W. SUNSET BLVD STE 315
WEST HOLLYWOOD CA 90069

Featured Artists Agency
8844 West Olympic Blvd., Suite 200
Beverly hills CA 90211

James Hirsen dba James Hirsen Talent Agency
505 South Villa Real Drive Suite 208
Anaheim Hills CA 92660

ELSA LORENA DE VEGA dba K MODEL AND
TALENT MANAG
1171 W. SHAW AVENUE #101
FRESNO CA 93711

THE STANDER GROUP, INC.
4533 VAN NUYS BLVD, SUITE 401
SHERMAN OAKS CA 91403

DANA RANDAZZO dba SYMBIOTIC TALENT
MANAGEMENT
714 E. VERDUGO #106   BURBANK CA 91501

HOLLYWOOD TALENT
AGENCY DIRECTORY

DIRECT2PRO, LLC dba D2 Models
1245 MCCLELLAN DRIVE #321
LOS ANGELES CA 90025

ARLENE WEISENBERG dba DAILY TALENT
AGENCY
11552 N. PEOMA PLACE #201
CHATSWORTH CA 91311

ARTISTIC TALENT, INC.
5437 LAUREL CANYON BLVD, SUITE 111
VALLEY VILLAGE CA 91607

DPN TALENT, INC.
9201 W. OLYMPIC BLVD
BEVERLY HILLS CA 90212

DOUG APATOW AGENCY, INC.
10559 Blythe Avenue
Los Angeles CA 90064

EASTERN TALENT AGENCY, LLC
1645 Vine St. # 402
LOS ANGELES CA 90028

LAURENCE S. BECSEY dba BECSEY
WISDOM KALAJIAN
12400 Wilshire Boulevard, Suite 500
LOS ANGELES CA 90025

HOLLYWOOD TALENT
AGENCY DIRECTORY

REFRESH TALENT AGENCY, INC.
24632 LA PLATA
LAGUNA NIGUEL CA 92677

THE KAPLAN-STAHLER AGENCY, INC.
8383 WILSHIRE BLVD #923
BEVERLY HILLS CA 90211

Vic Sutton-Dick Barth-Rita Vennari Agency, Inc
5900 Wilshire Blvd Suite 700
Los Angeles CA 90036

JE TALENT, LLC
155 Montgomery Street, Suite 805
SAN FRANCISCO CA 94104

MANNEQUIN MODELS
3540 OCEAN VIEW AVENUE
LOS ANGELES CA 90066

POWER TALENT GROUP
9465 WILSHIRE BLVD #300
BEVERLY HILLS CA 90212

GLOBAL ARTISTS AGENCY, LLC
6253 HOLLYWOOD BLVD, SUITE 508
LOS ANGELES CA 90028

REDPHIN PRODUCTIONS, LLC

HOLLYWOOD TALENT
AGENCY DIRECTORY

45 MALLORCA
LAGUNA NIGUEL CA 92677

SYLVARIA dba NEUMODELS
5348 VEGAS DRIVE # 1411
LAS VEGAS NV 89108

DIGITAL ARTISTS AGENCY, INC.
10101 Galaxy Way Bldg #3
LOS ANGELES CA 90067

FIRST ARTISTS MANAGEMENT
4764 PARK GRANADA, SUITE 110
CALABASAS CA 91302

ZPPA, INC
4929 WILSHIRE BLVD #808
LOS ANGELES CA 90010

THE HOWARD ROSE AGENCY
9460 WILSHIRE BLVD
BEVERLY HILLS CA 90212

ABOUT ENTERTAINMENT LLC
1207 WEST MAGNOLIA BLVD, SUITE D
BURBANK CA 91506

ENGAGE ARTISTS AGENCY INC

HOLLYWOOD TALENT
AGENCY DIRECTORY

1901 Avenue of the Stars #288
Los Angeles CA 90067

FAMOUS FRAMES, INC.
11124 Washington Blvd.
CULVER CITY CA 90232

BODY PARTS MODELS, INC.
5225 WILSHIRE BLVD #436
LOS ANGELES CA 90036

PAM PAHNKE dba Elegance Talent Agency
2763 STATE STREET
CARLSBAD CA 92008

AIM ARTISTS AGENCY, LLC
10846 BAIRD AVENUE
NORTHRIDGE CA 91326

SCOUT TALENT MANAGEMENT LLC
81 Lansing Street, Suite 401
SAN FRANCISCO CA 94105

SPIN ARTIST AGENCY, INC.
8335 W. SUNSET BLVD, SUITE 200
LOS ANGELES CA 90069

HOLLYWOOD TALENT
AGENCY DIRECTORY

H. DAVID MOSS
6063 VINELAND AVENUE, SUITE B
NORTH HOLLYWOOD CA 91606

STEPHEN G. MARISCAL
17620 SHERMAN WAY #213
VAN NUYS CA 91406

BERNICE H. HANSEN dba SPECTRUM LA
9107 WILSHIRE BLVD, STE 450
BEVERLY HILLS CA 90210

Karl B. Sanger dba Sanger Talent Agency
121 N. Harbor Blvd., Suite A
Fullerton CA 92832

MEMBRAIN, LLC
1800 CENTURY PARK EAST, SUITE 1000
LOS ANGELES CA 90067

Leavitt Agency Corporation dba JEFFREY
LEAVITT AG
11500 W. Olympic Blvd., #400
Los Angeles CA 90064

SPYROS SKOURAS, INC. dba Murtha Skouras
Agency
1025 Colorado Avenue
Santa Monica CA 90401

HOLLYWOOD TALENT
AGENCY DIRECTORY

Agency for the Performing Arts, LLC dba APA
405 S. Beverly Drive
Beverly Hills CA 90212

Bollotta & Associates, Inc dba Bollotta Enterta
2729 4th Avenue, Suite 1
San Diego CA 92103

APRIL ELIZABETH RAPP dba FOXXX
MODELING
20821 DEARBORNE STREET
CHATSWORTH CA 91311
KELLY CO, INC. dba SIGNATURE
ENTERTAINMENT LITERA
8306 WILSHIRE BLVD, SUITE 791
BEVERLY HILLS CA 90211

HERB TANNEN dba HERB TANNEN &
ASSOCIATES
20520 Pinnacle Way
Malibu CA 90265

MICHAEL WALLACH
908 GRANVILLE AVE., STE. 3
LOS ANGELES CA 90049

MAZLEA TALENT AGENCY LLC
7409 BEVERLY BLVD
LOS ANGELES CA 90036

HOLLYWOOD TALENT
AGENCY DIRECTORY

THE GERSH AGENCY, INC.
9465 WILSHIRE BLVD, 6TH FLOOR
BEVERLY HILLS CA 90212

M.O. ARTIST AGENCY, LLC
21900 BURBANK BLVD., SUITE 300
WOODLAND HILLS CA 91367

DEFINING ARTISTS, INC.
8721 Sunset Boulevard, Suite 209
West Hollywood CA 90069

JOEL KING dba PAKULA KING &
ASSOCIATES
9229 SUNSET BLVD., #400
LOS ANGELES CA 90069

ABOVE THE LINE AGENCY, INC.
468 N. CAMDEN DR. #200
BEVERLY HILLS CA 90210

JAY SIEGAN PRESENTS, LLC dba JAY
SIEGAN PRESENTS
1655 POLK ST., #1
SAN FRANCISCO CA 94109

WALTER D. SHAW III AND WALTER D. SHAW
JR. dba A.M
121 W. LEXINGTON DRIVE
GLENDALE CA 91203

HOLLYWOOD TALENT
AGENCY DIRECTORY

ZURI MODEL AND TALENT AGENCY, INC.
1999 AVENUE OF THE STARS, SUITE 1100
LOS ANGELES CA 90067

DON BUCHWALD & ASSOCIATES, INC.
5900 WILSHIRE BLVD., #3100
LOS ANGELES CA 90036

STEPHEN D. LINETT dba THE LINETTWORK
1901 AVENUE OF THE STARS, SUITE 1100
LOS ANGELES CA 90067

PHOTOGENICS TALENT LLC
3103A SOUTH LA CIENEGA BLVD
LOS ANGELES CA 90016

JC TALENT AGENCY, LLC dba JAGER
CAMPBELL TALENT A
201 N Brand Blvd Suite 200
Glendale CA 91203

The Happen Agency, LLC
7220 Owensmouth Ave., #220B
Canoga Park CA 91303

Christina Aude' dba Star Touch Agency
1545 Wilcox Ave Suite 201

HOLLYWOOD TALENT
AGENCY DIRECTORY

Los Angeles CA 90028

Preferred Artists, Inc.
16633 Ventura Blvd., Suite 1421
Encino CA 91436

XPOSE ENTERTAINMENT INC.
1055 E. COLORADO BLVD, 5TH FLOOR
PASADENA CA 91106

Stacy SOLODKIN dba Beth Stein & Associates
925 N. La Brea Ave 4th Fl.
Los Angeles CA 90038

Halcyon Talent, LLC
3500 West Olive Avenue
Burbank CA 91505

8x10 Models LLC
1261 Locust Street #95
Walnut Creek CA 94596

Panacea Entertainment Management
2021 Vista Alcedo
Camarillo CA 93012

RICHARD JOSEPH MAKAREWICZ dba APEX
TALENT GROUP
8383 WILSHIRE BLVD., STE. 800

HOLLYWOOD TALENT
AGENCY DIRECTORY

BEVERLY HILLS CA 90211

Greta M. Hanley dba BiCoastal Talent
2600 W Olive Ave., Ste. 500
Burbank CA 91505

SOVEREIGN TALENT GROUP, INC.
1642 WESTWOOD BLVD, SUITE 202
LOS ANGELES CA 90024

Tim O'Brien and Associates, Inc dba Clear
Talent
10950 Ventura Blvd.
Studio City CA 91604

FEATURED ARTISTS AGENCY
8844 W. OLYMPIC BLVD, SUITE 200
BEVERLY HILLS CA 90212

PARTISAN ARTS, INC.
1505 BRIDGEWAY, SUITE 205
SAUSALITO CA 94965

Kamstar Artist Management LLC dba Kamstar
Enterta
1896 Pacific Ave., #106
San Francisco CA 94109

RICHARD BAUMAN & ASSOCIATES, INC.
dba BRS/GAGE TA

HOLLYWOOD TALENT AGENCY DIRECTORY

6300 WILSHIRE BLVD., SUITE 1430   LOS ANGELES CA 90036

ASAP ACQUISITIONS SERVICES AND PROCUREMENTS, INC.
27955 Smyth Drive, Suite 103
VALENCIA CA 91355

DRAMATIC ARTISTS AGENCY, LA LLC
103 W. ALAMEDA AVENUE #139
BURBANK CA 91502

TWENTIETH CENTURY ARTISTS, INC.
19528 VENTURA BLVD, SUITE 612
TARZANA CA 91356

MODEL MANAGEMENT AGENCY, INC.
2635 CAMINO DEL RIO SOUTH, SUITE 202
SAN DIEGO CA 92108

TELLAVISION AGENCY, L.L.C.
1060 20TH STREET #8
SANTA MONICA CA 90403

Caroline Park dba Park Artists Group
14626 Magnolia Blvd., #4
Sherman Oaks CA 91403

HOLLYWOOD TALENT
AGENCY DIRECTORY

Evolution Music Partners, LLC
650 S. Grand Avenue, Suite 901
Los Angeles CA 90017

CREATIVE ARTISTS AGENCY, LLC
2000 AVENUE OF THE STARS
LOS ANGELES CA 90067

INNOVATIVE ARTISTS COMEDY DIVISION,
1505 TENTH STREET
SANTA MONICA CA 90401

APRIL MILLS ENTERTAINMENT LLC
10725 ACAMA STREET, APT 14
NORTH HOLLYWOOD CA 91602

MODEL TWO MANAGEMENT, LLLC
8000 SUNSET BLVD., STE #A201
LOS ANGELES CA 90046

ESSENTIAL ARTIST GROUP AGENCY, LLC
22231 MULHOLLAND HWY, SUITE 112A
CALABASAS CA 91302

BARRY PERELMAN ENTERPRISE, INC.
4237 VIA MARINA, SUITE J203
MARINA DEL REY CA 90292

NYLO MODEL & TALENT AGENCY, INC

HOLLYWOOD TALENT
AGENCY DIRECTORY

2121 N. California Boulevard, Suite 290
Walnut Creek CA 94596

VALERIE GREENBAUM dba EIGER ARTISTS
AGENCY
2464 PESQUERA DRIVE
LOS ANGELES CA 90049

AVANT ARTISTS LLC
21300 VICTORY BLVD. #505
WOODLAND HILLS CA 91367

MINC TALENT, LLC
7083 HOLLYWOOD BLVD., FOURTH FLOOR
LOS ANGELES CA 90028

ELIZABETH C. ST. DENIS dba ELIZABETH
ST. DENIS/AR
4032 Wilshire Blvd. #403
LOS ANGELES CA 90010

90210 TALENT INC.
16430 VENTURA BLVD., SUITE 200
ENCINO CA 91436

WILHELMINA WEST, INC.
9378 WILSHIRE BLVD., SUITE 310
BEVERLY HILLS CA 90212

HOLLYWOOD TALENT
AGENCY DIRECTORY

NEXXXT LEVEL TALENT AGENCY LLC
21501 Roscoe Blvd, Unit 120
Canoga Park CA 91304

HENDERSON REPRESENTS, INC.
11846 VENTURA BLVD., #302
STUDIO CITY CA 91604

JE MODEL MANAGEMENT, INC.
155 Montgomery Street, Suite 805
SAN FRANCISCO CA 94104

BRAD MADISON AND CHRISTOPHER
FAVILLE dba MONGREL
743 CENTER BLVD.
FAIRFAX CA 94930

W 1, INC. dba APERTURE TALENT
9378 WILSHIRE BLVD., SUITE 310
BEVERLY HILLS CA 90212

EXPECTING MODELS, INC.
21243 VENTURA BLVD., STE. 128
WOODLAND HILLS CA 91364

THE CULBERTSON GROUP, LLC
9107 WILSHIRE BLVD. #450
BEVERLY HILLS CA 90210

HOLLYWOOD TALENT
AGENCY DIRECTORY

TERESA H. REILLY & JULIE LYNNE
10725 VANOWEN ST., STE. 113
NORTH HOLLYWOOD CA 91505

NATURAL TALENT, INC.
3331 OCEAN PARK BLVD. #203
SANTA MONICA CA 90405

Mary Joy Guzman dba Wynn Star Production
828 Lakehaven Drive
Sunnyvale CA 94089

CLAIRE BEST & ASSOCIATES
736 SEWARD ST.
LOS ANGELES CA 90038

DreamRay Model and Talent Agency, LLC
5151 California Avenue, Suite 100
Irvine CA 92617

WARDEN, WHITE & ASSOCIATES
10866 Wilshire Blvd #300
Los Angeles CA 90024

THE ACTORS' HOUSE, INC.
5717 VALERIE AVE., SUITE 100
WOODLAND HILLS CA 91367

VOICEOVER LA, INC. dba VOICEOVER LA

HOLLYWOOD TALENT
AGENCY DIRECTORY

14144 VENTURA BLVD., SUITE 303
SHERMAN OAKS CA 91423

DONNA H. LEE dba CIRCLE TALENT
ASSOCIATES TALENT
401 WILSHIRE BLVD., 12TH FLOOR
PENTHOUSE
SANTA MONICA CA 90401

SHIRLEY WILSON & ASSOC., INC.
14140 VENTURA BLVD. STE. 206
SHERMAN OAKS CA 91423

BUSINESS MANAGEMENT LAB, INC.
10330 PIONEER BLVD., SUITE 250
SANTA FE SPRINGS CA 90670

NEWMARK MODELS INC. dba newMARK
Models
7083 HOLLYWOOD BLVD., 5TH FLOOR
LOS ANGELES CA 90028

WORLD PREMIER AGENCY, LLC
1015 12TH STREET, SUITE 10
MODESTO CA 95354

JAMES LUKANIK dba HUXLEY
ENTERTAINMENT MANAGEMENT
1265 1/2 HAVENHURST DR.
WEST HOLLYWOOD CA 90046

HOLLYWOOD TALENT
AGENCY DIRECTORY

ARETE TALENT AGENCY, LLC
454 N ROBERTSON BLVD., STE #1
WEST HOLLYWOOD CA 90048

ROTHMAN BRECHER LLC dba Rothman
Brecher Ehrich Li
9250 WILSHIRE BLVD., PENTHOUSE
BEVERLY HILLS CA 90212

METROPOLIS ANIMATION, INC.
9230 W. OLYMPIC BLVD., STE. 202
BEVERLY HILLS CA 90212

MARI SMITH PRESENTS, INC. dba MARY
SMITH PRESENTS
101 STATE PLACE, SUITE D
ESCONDIDO CA 92029

DDO ARTISTS AGENCY, LLC
4605 LANKERSHIM BLVD., SUITE #340
NORTH HOLLYWOOD CA 91602

8x10 MODELS LLC
166 GEARY STREET, SUITE 705
SAN FRANCISCO CA 94108

HOLLYWOOD TALENT
AGENCY DIRECTORY

OURTNEY HANLON dba HANLON TALENT
AGENCY
6210 WILSHIRE BLVD., #305
LOS ANGELES CA 90048

HABER ENTERTAINMENT
434 S. CANON DR., SUITE 204
BEVERLY HILLS CA 90212

SHANNON MICHELLE LOAR-COTE dba
HELLO GORGEOUS MOD
108 WEST MISSION UNIT B
SANTA BARBARA CA 93101

SHIRLEY ANN WILSON dba WILSON &
ASSOCIATES
6472 SANTA MONICA BLVD.
HOLLYWOOD CA 90038

JENNY NARCISA STRICKLIN dba JENNY
STRICKLIN TALEN
1438 N. Gower St. Bldg 2 - Rm 39
HOLLYWOOD CA 90028

Genetic Models Management, LLC
1601, N Gower st
Los angeles CA 90028

HOLLYWOOD TALENT
AGENCY DIRECTORY

Genetic Models Management, LLC
1601, N Gower st
Los angeles CA 90028

AHLIA DEMAS JIMENEZ dba AhhFlee
Productions
1918 Fairway Circle DriveLake
San Marcos CA 92078

FREEDOM 6.21, INC. dba SOLO ARTISTS
2251 Guthrie Circle
Los Angeles CA 90034

DIRECT MODELS, INC. dba LA DIRECT
MODELS
770 L STREET, SUITE 950
SACRAMENTO CA 95814

HTG ARTISTS, LLC dba ESTEEMED
ARTISTS TALENT AGEN
4150 W. RIVERSIDE DR. #206
BURBANK CA 91505

NEJ, LTD dba BRESLER KELLY &
ASSOCIATES
11500 W OLYMPIC BLVD. #400
LOS ANGELES CA 90064

HOLLYWOOD TALENT
AGENCY DIRECTORY

REVA, LTD. dba CHEZ CHIC TALENT
850 EAST OCEAN BLVD. #1209
LONG BEACH CA 90802

TODD SHEMARYA ARTISTS, INC.
2550 OUTPOST DR.
LOS ANGELES CA 90068

Epic Media Consulting, LLC
6085 Calle Camposeco
Rancho Santa Fe CA 92067

ROBERT EMMANUEL DEPPE dba BEVERLY
HECHT AGENCY
12100 WILSHIRE BLVD., SUITE 800
LOS ANGELES CA 90025

TAMBELLINI PRODUCTIONS, INC. dba THE
EVENT CONSUL
188 E. 17TH ST., SUITE 204
COSTA MESA CA 92627

INNOVATIVE ARTISTS
1505 TENTH STREET
SANTA MONICA CA 90401

GENETIC MODELS MANAGEMENT, LLC

HOLLYWOOD TALENT
AGENCY DIRECTORY

6201 HOLLYWOOD BLVD.
LOS ANGELES CA 90028

PATRIK SIMPSON dba NETWORK
INTERNATIONAL MODELS A
275 SOUTH BEVERLY DRIVE STE. 215
BEVERLY HILLS CA 90210

LARCHMONT LITERARY AGENCY, INC.
444 N. LARCHMONT BLVD. #200
LOS ANGELES CA 90004

ABSTRACT TALENT, INC.
5023 N. PARKWAY
CALABASAS CA 91302

CHARLOTTE M. WILD dba SIRENA MODELS
332 S. BEVERLY DRIVE #100
BEVERLY HILLS CA 90212

ROBERT ANDREW SALTZBURG dba RC
TALENT AGENCY
9020 BEVERLY BLVD., #PENTHOUSE
WEST HOLLYWOOD CA 90048

MELODY LOMBOY AND THOMAS E. LOWE
dba L&L TALENT

HOLLYWOOD TALENT
AGENCY DIRECTORY

416 MALAGA LANE #C
PALOS VERDES ESTATES CA 90274

SMS TALENT, INC.
8383 WILSHIRE BLVD. #230
BEVERLY HILLS CA 90211

WORK TALENT LLC
21747 ERWIN STREET, 2ND FLOOR
WOODLAND HILLS CA 91367

BONITA ELLEN HART dba AVENUE ACTORS
AGENCY
12435 OXNARD ST.
NORTH HOLLYWOOD CA 91606

Caryn Sterling
28912 Roadside Drive
Agoura Hills CA 91301

MARY JOY GUZMAN dba WYNN STAR
PRODUCTION AND TALE
828 LAKEHAVEN DR.
SUNNYVALE CA 94089

SPORTS UNLIMITED TALENT AGENCY, INC.
dba Sports a

HOLLYWOOD TALENT
AGENCY DIRECTORY

7080 HOLLYWOOD BLVD., SUITE 306
LOS ANGELES CA 90028

MOSS MODELS, LLC
8033 W. SUNSET BLVD, #804
LOS ANGELES CA 90046

FREEDOM MODELS CALIFORNIA, INC.
820 N. FAIRFAX AVE.
WEST HOLLYWOOD CA 90046

NIKKIZ ANGELS, INC. dba EXCELSIOR
TALENT
7204 LITTLER CT.
MOORPARK CA 93021

The Asiano Agency, LLC dba
UmbrellaGirlsUSA
347 W I Street
Encinitas CA

DENNIS\KARG & COMPANY, INC. dba FILM
ARTISTS ASSO
21044 VENTURA BLVD., #215
WOODLAND HILLS CA 91364

Era Talent Agency LLC

HOLLYWOOD TALENT
AGENCY DIRECTORY

714 North La Brea #240
Los Angeles CA 90038

International Idols Agency, LLC
641 N. Larchmont Blvd., 777
Los Angeles CA 90004
DESIREE LAVONNE PARKER ADKISON dba
LAVONNE'S THE
7255 INDEPENDENCE AVENUE, SUITE 308
CANOGA PARK CA 91303-3695

GRAY TALENT GROUP, INC.
15315 Magnolia Boulevard, Unit 203
Sherman Oaks CA 91403

SHARON CARRY dba CARRY COMPANY
3875 WILSHIRE BLVD , #402
LOS ANGELES CA 90010

BARON ENTERTAINMENT, INC. dba BARON
ENTERTAINMENT
13848 VENTURA BLVD, SUITE A
SHERMAN OAKS CA 91423

KARL HOFHEINZ dba SYNERGY TALENT
GROUP
13251 VENTURA BLVD #2
STUDIO CITY CA 91604

THE BRODER/KURLAND AGENCY, INC.
11400 W. OLYMPIC BLVD, SUITE 590

HOLLYWOOD TALENT
AGENCY DIRECTORY

LOS ANGELES CA 90064

VARIETY ARTIST INTERNATIONAL, INC.
1111 RIVERSIDE DRIVE, SUITE 501
PASO ROBLES CA 93446

VINCE SPADEA dba VINCE MODELS
100 N DOHNEY DRIVE, SUITE 104
LOS ANGELES CA 90048

GO 2 TALENT AGENCY, INC.
2825 W MAGNOLIA BLVD
BURBANK CA 91505

JANA LUKER dba JANA LUKER AGENCY
20501 VENTURA BLVD, SUITE 115
WOODLAND HILLS CA 91364

ESPRIT TALENT AGENCY
11620 WILSHIRE BLVD., 9TH FLOOR
LOS ANGELES CA 90025

WHAMI HWANG dba FAME TALENT AGENCY
1441 N. MCCADEN PLACE
LOS ANGELES CA 90046

HOLLYWOOD TALENT
AGENCY DIRECTORY

RAUL SARMIENTO VEGA dba CHINO
AGENCY GROUP
14083 SAN ANTONIO AVENUE
CHINO CA 91710

ELEV8, LLC
489 S, ROBERTSON BLVD, SUITE 206
BEVERLY HILLS CA 90211

JAIME R. COTA ET AL
9430 OLYMPIC BLVD
BEVERLY HILLS CA 90212

VICTOR KRUGLOV
6565 SUNSET BLVD, SUITE 300
LOS ANGELES CA 90028

RACHEL YVONNE JOHNSTON dba
COVENANT CREATIVE GROU
1055 7TH STREET, FLOOR 33
LOS ANGELES CA 90017

TWILIGHT TALENT AGENCY, LLC
5250 Lankershim Boulevard, #500
North Hollywood CA 91601

JORDAN MCKIRAHAN dba JORDAN
MCKIRAHAN TALENT AGEN
6303 OWENSMOUTH AVE., STE 1032

HOLLYWOOD TALENT
AGENCY DIRECTORY

WOODLAND HILLS CA 91367

TRACI ANN HALVORSON dba HALVORSON
MODEL MANAGEMENT
3777 STEVENS CREEK BLVD, SUITE 440
SANTA CLARA CA 95051

INTERNATIONAL CREATIVE MANAGEMENT
PARTNERS LLC
10250 CONSTELLATION BOULEVARD
LOS ANGELES CA 90067

THOMAS JESSE GOFF
386 S. BURNSIDE AVENUE - Suite 4F
LOS ANGELES CA 90036

CIRCLE OF 10 TALENT
333 EL CAMINO REAL, SUITE 200
TUSTIN CA 92780

HIP ENTERTAINMENT, LLC
7277 LONE PINE DRIVE, SUITE 201
RANCHO MURIETA CA 95683

BETH BOHN MANAGEMENT, INC.
2420 LAKE VIEW AVENUE
LOS ANGELES CA 90039

HOLLYWOOD TALENT
AGENCY DIRECTORY

TOAY LYNN FOSTER-ORTIZ & GEORGE JAD
YAZBECK
3481 OLD CONEJO ROAD, SUITE 103
NEWBURY PARK CA 91320

Adam Sinjin Park dba Park Noack Agency
10866 Wilshire Boulevard, Suite 400
Los Angeles CA 90024

TALENT BRANDED ENTERTAINMENT, INC.
14724 VENTURA BLVD, PENTHOUSE
SHERMAN OAKS CA 91403

SHARON KEMP dba SHARON KEMP TALENT
AGENCY/KEMP KO
865 COMSTOCK AVENUE, #11C
LOS ANGELES CA 90024

VIC SUTTON-DICK BARTH-RITA VENNARI
AGENCY, INC.
5900 WILSHIRE BLVD, SUITE 700
LOS ANGELES CA 90036

HARMONY ARTISTS, INC.
3575 CAHUENGA BLVD. W #560
LOS ANGELES CA 90068

HOLLYWOOD TALENT
AGENCY DIRECTORY

AMELIA AGENCY, INC. dba GREYSCALE
MGMT dba CLOUT
8952 ELLIS AVENUE
LOS ANGELES CA 90034

KELLY D. ALLRED dba TOP NOTCH TALENT,
TALENT AGEN
524 S. CLOVIS AVENUE, SUITE N
FRESNO CA 93727

NATURAL MODEL MANAGEMENT, LLC
1120 N. EL CENTRO AVENUE, #9
LOS ANGELES CA 90038

PHOTOGENICS MEDIA LLC
3103A S. LA CIENEGA BLVD
LOS ANGELES CA 90016

ALLEGRO TALENT GROUP, LLC
3445 RIDGEFORD DRIVE
WESTLAKE VILLAGE CA 91361

RICHARD A. DELANCY
3733 E. COLORADO STREET
LONG BEACH CA 90814

HOLLYWOOD TALENT
AGENCY DIRECTORY

DAVID EISENBERG dba PROTEGE
ENTERTAINMENT
710 E. ANGELENO AVENUE
BURBANK CA 91501

VIRGINIA DIB dba MALAKY INTERNATIONAL
205 South Beverly Drive, Suite 211
Beverly Hills CA 90212

CROSBY CARTER MANAGEMENT, LLC
2463 Meadow Valley Terrace
Los Angeles CA 90039

BLOC TALENT AGENCY, INC.
1680 VINE ST., STE. 600
LOS ANGELES CA 90048

BOBBY GENE JUAREZ dba The Boss Booking
18119 S. PRAIRIE AVENUE
TORRANCE CA 90504

THE WAYNE AGENCY, LLC
3255 WILSHIRE BLVD, SUITE 1534
BEVERLY HILLS CA 90010

TROY BRONSTEIN dba T-BEST TALENT
AGENCY
3544 ARDEN ROAD

HOLLYWOOD TALENT
AGENCY DIRECTORY

HAYWARD CA 94545

SCOTT SCHWARTZ, INC. dba VISION ART
MANAGEMENT
9465 WILSHIRE BLVD., STE. 870
BEVERLY HILLS CA 90212

KOR Talent Agency LLC
120 S. Victory Blvd., #202
Burbank CA 91502

THE CONCERT AGENCY, LLC
1301 Montana Avenue Suite B
SANTA MONICA CA 90403

ASHLEY NOELLE MAYER dba LEGEND 3
ENTERTAINMENT
21243 VENTURA BLVD, SUITE 102
WOODLAND HILLS CA 91364

HOLLYWOOD MODEL MANAGEMENT, INC.
dba HOLLYWOOD SE
8744 HOLLOWAY DRIVE
WEST HOLLYWOOD CA 90069

CAMILLE SORICE dba CAMILLE SORICE
AGENCY
19710 VENTURA BLVD, #104
WOODLAND HILLS CA 91364

HOLLYWOOD TALENT
AGENCY DIRECTORY

RAIN TALENT LLC
1547 14TH STREET
SANTA MONICA CA 90404

SOUNDTRACK MUSIC ASSOCIATES, LLC
4133 REDWOOD AVENUE, SUITE 3030
LOS ANGELES CA 90066

GILBERT INSURANCE SERVICES, INC.
TALENT AGENCY
9454 Wilshire Blvd. Suite 510
BEVERLY HILLS CA 90212

CHRISTINA WALKER dba CA TALENT
9936 ROBBINS DRIVE
BEVERLY HILLS CA 90212

ARLENE THORNTON & ASSOCIATES, INC.
12711 VENTURA BLVD, #490
STUDIO CITY CA 91604

AESIR TALENT, LLC
7032 WILBUR AVENUE
RESEDA CA 91335

DAIRY A. VERAS REEVES dba UNIVERSAL
TALENT AGENCY
4221 Wilshire Blvd Suite 290
Los Angeles CA 90010

HOLLYWOOD TALENT
AGENCY DIRECTORY

Janet Lee Robinson dba Choyce International
Plus
4104 Singing Tree Way
Antelope CA 95843

SUZAN ROLLINS dba TITANIA
ENTERTAINMENT
5678 SLICERS CIRCLE
AGOURA HILLS CA 91301

ELLIS TALENT GROUP
4705 LAUREL CANYON BLVD., #300
VALLEY VILLAGE CA 91607

Hot Shot Management Inc.
1055 W 1st st # E
Santa Ana CA 92703

3 ARTIST MANAGEMENT
2800 OLYMPIC BLVD, 2ND FLR
SANTA MONICA CA 90404

LAYA GELFF METZGER dba LAYA GELFF
AGENCY
16133 VENTURA BLVD, SUITE 700
ENCINO CA 91436

HOLLYWOOD TALENT
AGENCY DIRECTORY

THE GLICK AGENCY, LLC
5400 LINDLEY AVENUE, #112A
ENCINO CA 91316

ELITE MODEL MANAGEMENT LA, LLC
518 North La Cienega Boulevard
West Hollywood CA 90048

IF MANAGEMENT, INC.
152 WEST 57TH STREET, FLOOR 19
NEW YORK NY 10019

Brick Entertainment, LLC dba BrickHouse
Talent d
18663 Ventura Blvd, Suite 201
Tarzana CA 91356

STARWIL REED & GWEN REED dba
STARWIL PRODUCTIONS
433 N. CAMDEN DRIVE, 4TH FLOOR
BEVERLY HILLS CA 90210

THOSE OTHER PLACE TALENT AGENCY,
10545 BURBANK BLVD, SUITE 112
NORTH HOLLYWOOD CA 91601

Team Duswalt, Inc. dba PEAK MODELS &
TALENT
280 N. Westlake Blvd., Suite 110
Westlake Village CA 91362

HOLLYWOOD TALENT
AGENCY DIRECTORY

P. Parsons Company, Inc.
37 Quail Court #101
Walnut Creek CA 94596

STUART M. MILLER dba THE STUART M.
MILLER CO.
11684 VENTURA BLVD, SUITE 225
STUDIO CITY CA 91604

THE SCHRAMM GROUP LLC dba THE
SCHRAMM GROUP
4464 Bergamo Drive
Encino   CA 91436

INCITE MANAGEMENT INC.
22468 PAUL REVERE DRIVE
CALABASAS CA 91302

JOE KOLKOWITZ dba PLAYERS TALENT
AGENCY
16130 VENTURA BLVD, SUITE 235
ENCINO CA 91436

ALCHEMY BY FAUST, LLC
1375 COLE ROAD
AROMAS CA 95004

HOLLYWOOD TALENT
AGENCY DIRECTORY

GORO HAMASAKI dba East Group Agency
14545 FRIAR STREET, SUITE 101
VAN NUYS CA 91411

ELTON BOLDEN dba Tilmar Talent Agency
6404 WILSHIRE BLVD, SUITE 735
LOS ANGELES CA 90048

Firestarter Entertainment, LLC dba
FIRESTARTER EN
21550 Oxnard Street, Suite 300
Woodland Hills   CA 91367

JONATHAN CALEB DONNER dba THUNDER
TALENT AGENCY
910 HAMPSHIRE RD., STE. R
WESTLAKE VILLAGE CA 91361

WILSON EVENTS, INC.
515 B STREET
PETALUMA CA 94952

INSPIRATION NATION PRODUCTIONS, INC.
1111 E. RAMON RD., UNIT #10
PALM SPRINGS CA 92264

THE MODEL SMITH, LLC
1055 W 7TH ST., 33FL/PH
LOS ANGELES CA 90017

HOLLYWOOD TALENT
AGENCY DIRECTORY

MODELS INC TALENT AGENCY
264 SPRING STREET
PLEASANTON CA 94566

JONATHAN DAVID FINBERG dba FIRST
ROW TALENT
4735 Sepulveda Boulevard, #221
Sherman Oaks CA 91403

KKS PRODUCTIONS, LLC dba KOSPRE
8316 MELROSE AVE.
LOS ANGELES CA 90069

MARLENE MARIE HARTJE dba THE
MARLENE AGENCY
6080 CENTER DR., 6TH FLOOR
LOS ANGELES CA 90045

BMG TALENT GROUP, INC.
5455 WILSHIRE BLVD., SUITE 900
LOS ANGELES CA 90036   I

BENSIMON MODELS AND TALENT, LLC
11665 AVENA PLACE, #205
SAN DIEGO CA 92128

HOLLYWOOD TALENT
AGENCY DIRECTORY

ALBERT EUGENE BENDER & CHRISTOPHER
JAMES BENDER
7080 HOLLYWOOD BLVD, SUITE 1100
LOS ANGELES CA 90028

101 MODELING
24372 VANOWEN STREET, SUITE 206
WEST HILLS CA 91307

GRANT, SAVIC, KOPALOFF & ASSOCIATES,
LLC
4929 WILSHIRE BLVD, SUITE 259
LOS ANGELES CA 90010

KP PRODUCTIONS, INC. dba KELLY
PRODUCTIONS
824 MUNRAS AVENUE, SUITE D
MONTEREY CA 93940

Bagula Riviere Coates and Associates, LLP
9888 Carroll Centre Road, Suite 235
San Diego CA 92126

BERMAN/SACKS TALENT AGENCY LLC
2600 WEST OLIVE AVE., STE. 500
BURBANK CA 91505

HOLLYWOOD TALENT
AGENCY DIRECTORY

INTRINSIC LLC
8335 SUNSET BLVD, SUITE 301
WEST HOLLYWOOD CA 90069

LoveStone Talent Agency, LLC
145 S. Fairfax Ave., Suite 200
Los Angeles CA 90036

P. PARSONS COMPANY, INC.
1630 N. MAIN ST. #412
WALNUT CREEK CA 94596

STEVEN STEVENS dba THE STEVENS
GROUP
14011 VENTURA BLVD., SUITE 200
SHERMAN OAKS CA 91423

MICHAEL R. LEWIS dba MICHAEL LEWIS &
ASSOCIATES
2506 FIFTH STREET, SUITE 100
SANTA MONICA CA 90405

GREEN LIGHT TALENT AGENCY, INC.
2811 WILSHIRE BLVD, SUITE 570
SANTA MONICA CA 90403

HOLLYWOOD TALENT
AGENCY DIRECTORY

SANDRA BROSNAN dba ONEWORLD MODEL
AND TALENT
2127 LINNINGTON AVENUE
LOS ANGELES CA 90025

THE CANDACE LAKE AGENCY, INC.
1072 LAUREL LANE
PEBBLE BEACHCA 93953

INNOVATIVE ARTISTS TALENT AND
LITERARY AGENCY, INC
1505 10TH ST
SANTA MONICA CA 90401

PAUL JONATHAN STROTHEIDE dba JS
REPRESENTS
7805 SUNSET BLVD. #211
LOS ANGELES CA 90046

ZE ANIMATION STUDIOS INC.
9465 WILSHIRE BLVD. #300
BEVERLY HILLS CA 90212

AVO TALENT, INC.
5670 WILSHIRE BLVD, SUITE 1930
LOS ANGELES CA 90036

HOLLYWOOD TALENT
AGENCY DIRECTORY

STACHE, INC. dba M&M GROUP
16872 BOLSA CHICA ST., SUITE 204
HUNTINGTON BEACH CA 92649

VOX, INC.
6420 WILSHIRE BLVD., #1080
LOS ANGELES CA 90048

TALENTWORKS, INC.
3500 W. OLIVE AVENUE, SUITE 1400
BURBANK CA 91505

REBEL ENTERTAINMENT PARTNERS, INC.
5700 WILSHIRE BLVD, SUITE 470
LOS ANGELES CA 90036

GAIL SHERMAN JONES dba
TALENT+PLUS/LOS LATINOS TA
318 RHINE COURT
SALINAS CA 93906

High Road Touring, LLC
751 Bridgeway, 3rd Floor
Sausalito CA 94965

C & L Promotions, LLC
P O Box 386
Suisun City CA 94585-0386

HOLLYWOOD TALENT
AGENCY DIRECTORY

Dynamic Artists Management, LLC
5221 Central Avenue, Suite 202
Richmond CA 94804

THE ALPERN GROUP
15645 ROYAL OAK RD.
ENCINO CA 91436

VERVE TALENT AND LITERARY AGENCY,
LLC
6310 SAN VICENTE BLVD, SUITE 100
LOS ANGELES CA 90048

PAUL KOHNER INC. dba THE KOHNER
AGENCY
9300 WILSHIRE BLVD, SUITE 555
BEVERLY HILLS CA 90212

SUSAN COLLEEN DUFF & MARY KATHLEEN
SCHMIDT
2600 W. OLIVE AVENUT, 5TH FLOOR
BURBANK CA 91505

MDT TALENT AGENCY, INC. dba MARLA
DELL TALENT AGE
2124 UNION ST., SUITE C
SAN FRANCISCO CA 94123

HOLLYWOOD TALENT
AGENCY DIRECTORY

SASHA BOGIE, INC. dba NTA MODEL
MANAGEMENT
1445 N. STANLEY AVENUE, SUITE 200
LOS ANGELES CA 90046

GIANNELLI ENTERTAINMENT dba OMNIUM
ENTERTAINMENT
444 N. LARCHMONT BLVD., #105
LOS ANGELES CA 90004

CHAMPAGNE TROTT MANAGEMENT LLC
dba VISION MODELS
8631 WASHINGTON BLVD
CULVER CITY CA 90232

NTA TALENT AGENCY, INC. dba NTA
TALENT AGENCY
1445 N. STANLEY AVENUE, 2ND FLOOR
LOS ANGELES CA 90046

ELECTRA STAR MODELING AGENCY, LLC
9229 W SUNSET BLVD., SUITE 415
WEST HOLLYWOOD CA 90069

GERENCIA 360 MANAGEMENT, INC. dba
Gerencia 360 Ag
300 E MAGNOLIA BLVD., STE. 500
BURBANK CA 91502

HOLLYWOOD TALENT
AGENCY DIRECTORY

OC MODELING, LLC
22024 LASSEN ST., UNIT #114
CHATSWORTH CA 91311

NATURALLY FIT, LLC
7080 HOLLYWOOD BLVD. STE. 1100
LOS ANGELES CA 90028

BIGG TIME ENTERTAINMENT, INC.
14320 VENTURA BLVD., STE. 457
SHERMAN OAKS CA 91423

SAL REYES dba OTTO MODELS, TALENT
AGENCY
2901 W. COAST HWY. #350
NEWPORT BEACH CA 92663

Tangerine Talent LLC
15130 Ventura Blvd Suite 308
Sherman Oaks CA 91403

OSBRINK TALENT AGENCY INC dba
OSBRINK TALENT AGEN
2222 W. Olive Avenue
Burbank CA 91506

THE GREAT BALBOA, LLC dba THE ALL
AMERICAN RASCAL
4960 Woodruff Avenue
Lakewood CA 90713

HOLLYWOOD TALENT
AGENCY DIRECTORY

VIRGILIO GUILLEN dba MIRAMAR TALENT
AGENCY
9415 CULVER BLVD.
CULVER CITY CA 90232

THE INDUSTRY GROUP USA, LLC dba
Industry Model
469 S. Robertson Boulevard
Beverly Hills CA 90211

DANIEL HOFF AGENCY, INC.
5455 WILSHIRE BLVD, SUITE 1100
LOS ANGELES CA 90036

THE HOUSE OF REPRESENTATIVES, A
TALENT AGENCY Inc.
3118 Wilshire Boulevard, Unit D
Santa Monica CA 90403

PHILLIP L. BROCK dba Studio Talent Group
1328 12th Street, Ste. #2 and #3
Santa Monica CA 90401

THE ACOUSTIC SPOT LLC
445 MARINE VIEW AVE., STE. 300
DEL MAR CA 92014

HOLLYWOOD TALENT
AGENCY DIRECTORY

PARTOS AGENCY, LLC
247 Windward Avenue
Venice CA 90291

SDB PARTNERS, INC.
315 SOUTH BEVERLY DR., STE. 411
BEVERLY HILLS CA 90212

Volition Media Group LLC
21420 Peggy Joyce Ln
Santa Clarita CA 91350

MAGGIE MAY PRODUCTIONS LLC dba BLUE
MOON PRODUCTI
26421 DEER CREEK LANE
SANTA CLARITA CA 91387

IDEAL TALENT AGENCY LLC
10806 VENTURA BLVD., STE. 2
STUDIO CITY CA 91604

BRAD GELFOND dba STRIKE UP THE
BRAND
2034 Kerwood Avenue
Los Angeles CA 90025

BRAD GELFOND dba STRIKE UP THE
BRAND 321 S. PECK DR.
BEVERLY HILLS CA 90212

HOLLYWOOD TALENT
AGENCY DIRECTORY

SARAH DELANG KING dba LANG TALENT
621 VIA COLINAS BL67
WESTLAKE VILLAGE CA 91362

HARVEY LANCE MCMILLAN dba UNLIMITED
ENTERTAINMENT
1055 WEST 7TH ST. 33RD FLOOR 111
PENTHOUSE
LOS ANGELES CA 90017

William Whitfield and Lawrence Abramson
332 S Beverly Dr
Beverly Hills CA 90212

MITCHELL K. STUBBS & ASSOCIATES
8695 WEST WASHINGTON BLVD., STE. 204
CULVER CITY CA 90232

Patricia Brink dba Tricia Brink Management
2216 Ocean Park Blvd #A
Santa Monica CA 90405

SHAUNTIEL LINDSEY MILLER dba
SHAUNTIEL LINDSEY TA
8484 WILSHIRE BLVD. #515

Something LLC
2227 Mandeville Canyon Rd
Los Angeles CA 90049

HOLLYWOOD TALENT
AGENCY DIRECTORY

WORLDWIDE PRODUCTION AGENCY, LLC
144 N. ROBERTSON BLVD., STE. A
WEST HOLLYWOOD CA 90048

ZOHAL DARA TERANCHI dba OC TALENT
GROUP
5 Coachman
Dove Canyon CA 92679

ADAMS BROADCAST CONSULTING
17350 MALLARD DR.
SONOMA CA 95476

BRATTY MODEL, LLC
210 POST ST., STE. 1102
SAN FRANCISCO CA 94108

THE WEISS AGENCY, INC.
14954 CORONA DEL MAR
PACIFIC PALISADES CA 90272

COLLEEN CLER AGENCY
178 S. VICTORY BLVD. Ste. 108
BURBANK CA 91502

GM & D, INC. dba TGMD TALENT AGENCY
6767 FOREST LAWN DR. #206
LOS ANGELES CA 90068

HOLLYWOOD TALENT
AGENCY DIRECTORY

MONTEIRO ROSE DRAVIS AGENCY, INC.
dba THE DRAVIS
4370 TUJUNGA AVE., #145
STUDIO CITY CA 91604

MULTI PLATFORM MANAGEMENT
PARTNERS INC
527 W 7TH ST STE 800
LOS ANGELES CA 90014

THEODOSIA SHOR & LORI BREVIG dba NBS
ENTERTAINMEN
1230 CALLE SUERTE, SUITE A
CAMARILLO CA 93012

IDEAL IMAGE INTERNATIONAL CORP. dba
IDEAL IMAGE M
10827 Hortense Street, Suite 11
North Hollywood CA 91602

Skyn Talent LLC
7944 Nookfield Dr
Las Vegas NV 89147

ATEI COMPANY, INC. dba THAT'S
ENTERTAINMENT PRODU
3820 E. LA PALMA AVE.
ANAHEIM CA 92807

HOLLYWOOD TALENT
AGENCY DIRECTORY

THE CRITERION GROUP, INC. dba
CRITERION GROUP
4842 SYLMAR AVE.
SHERMAN OAKS CA 91423

CONCEPT TALENT GROUP, LLC dba
CONCEPT TALENT GROU
193 N. ROBERTSON BLVD.
BEVERLY HILLS CA 90211

ACTORS AND ARTISTS AGENCY
2443 NORTH NAOMI ST.
BURBANK CA 91504

DEBORAH LYNN PALMER BEAL dba BEAL
TALENT & ASSOCI
5850 Canoga Avenue 4th Floor
Woodland Hills CA 91367

MARIEL RIVERA dba THE REPUBLIC
AGENCY
4100 W. ALAMEDA AVE., SUITE 352
BURBANK CA 91505

THE VIP CONNECT, INC.
15206 VENTURA BLVD., #210
SHERMAN OAKS CA 91403

HOLLYWOOD TALENT
AGENCY DIRECTORY

BBA TALENT INC. dba BBA
3500 W. OLIVE AVE., STE. 300
BURBANK CA 91505

SECOND OCTAVE TALENT AGENCY, LLC
1400 VALLEY HOUSE DRIVE, SUITE 262
RONHERT PARK CA 94928

AMERICAN ARTISTS CORPORATION
8500 WILSHIRE BOULEVARD, #525
BEVERLY HILLS CA 90211

SAINT AGENCY INC
925 N LA BREA AVE 4TH FLOOR
LOS ANGELES CA 90038

ALVARADO REY AGENCY, INC.
7906 SANTA MONICA BLVD., #205
WEST HOLLYWOOD CA 90046

Bicoastal Models and Talent
8228 Sunset Blvd Ste. 313
West Hollywood CA 90046

Jeffrey W. Mayes dba M Talent
4335 Van Nuys Blvd., Suite 449
Sherman Oaks CA 91403

HOLLYWOOD TALENT
AGENCY DIRECTORY

CHRISTOPHER MAGGIORE dba ARTISTS
WORLDWIDE
3660 WILSHIRE BLVD., #1134
LOS ANGELES CA 90010

KEN LINDNER & ASSOCIATES, INC.
1901 Avenue of the Stars, Suite 1010
Los Angeles CA 90067

MEIYA TOKYO USA
4275 EXECUTIVE SQUARE, STE. 200
LA JOLLA CA 92037

Aaron Lindsay Jordan dba SKILD.
7755 Center Ave. Suite 1100
Huntington Beach CA 92647

TWOLA HEADS ENTERTAINMENT GROUP
7719 Somerset Blvd.
Paramount CA 90723

Entertainment Group International LLC.
9414 Dayton Way
Beverly Hills CA 90210

Valerie Emanuel dba Role Models Management
701 W Manchester Suite 204
Inglewood CA 90301

HOLLYWOOD TALENT
AGENCY DIRECTORY

O Models, Inc.
145 South Fairfax Ave., Ste. 200
Los Angeles CA 91602

STEPHEN JOHN VIEIRA dba SJV
ENTERPRISES & ASSOCIA
4025 BEETHOVEN STREET
MAR VISTA CA 90066

Entertainment Lab
8447 Wilshire Blvd. Suite 103
Beverly Hills CA 90211

INNOVATIVE ARTISTS BROADCAST
DIVISION LLC
1505 10TH STREET
SANTA MONICA CA 90401

Bell Talent, Inc.
40992 Calle Pueblo
Indio CA 92203

CARISSA MITCHELL dba MITCHELL &
ASSOCIATES TALENT
18356 OXNARD ST. #7
TARZANA CA 91356

GERMAN E. MORALES dba MGMT ARTISTS
1201 W 5TH ST., SUITE 180
LOS ANGELES CA 90017

HOLLYWOOD TALENT
AGENCY DIRECTORY

ROUGE ARTISTS, INC.
13428 Maxella Ave. Ste. 514
MARINA DEL REY CA 90292

LISA CALLAMARO dba LISA CALLAMARO
LITERARY AGENCY
427 N. CANON DR. #215
BEVERLY HILLS CA 90210

THE GYPSY SHACK
555 W 5TH ST., 35TH FLOOR
LOS ANGELES CA 90013

StatusSilver LLC
465 E Tujunga Ave #2
Burbank CA 91501

Stars, The Agency
23 Grant Avenue, 4th floor
San Francisco CA 94108

Domina Talent Agency LLC dba DTA
30700 Russell Ranch Road, Suite 250
Westlake Village CA 91362

MEDIA ARTISTS GROUP
8222 MELROSE AVE., SUITE 304
LOS ANGELES CA 90046

HOLLYWOOD TALENT
AGENCY DIRECTORY

VOICEOVER LA, INC. dba VOICEOVER LA
14144 VENTURA BLVD., SUITE 303
SHERMAN OAKS CA 91423

A4 AMELI ARTISTS AND ATHLETES
AGENCY, INC.
9171 WILSHIRE BLVD., STE. 380
BEVERLY HILLS CA 90210

DAY AFTER DAY PRODUCTIONS, INC.
1430 REMINGTON DR.
SANTA YNEZ CA 93460

TEC PRODUCTIONS, INC.
344 TULLY ROAD
SAN JOSE CA 95111

Be Social Public Relations LLC
2552 Gateway Road
Carlsbad CA 92009

REECE KAUANU TAGARA
3727 BUCHANAN STREET, 4TH FLOOR
SAN FRANCISCO CA 94123

DIVISION WEST MANAGEMENT, LLC dba
FRANK MODEL MAN
5600 AVENIDA
ENCINAS CA 92008

HOLLYWOOD TALENT
AGENCY DIRECTORY

BRANT ROSE dba BRANT ROSE AGENCY
6671 SUNSET BLVD., STE. 1584B
LOS ANGELES CA 90028

MURTHA SKOURAS AGENCY
1025 COLORADO AVE., SUITE B
SANTA MONICA CA 90401

Nu Talent Agency, Inc.
117 N Robertson Blvd
Los Angeles CA 90048

MUSIC ZIRCONIA, INC.
5595 MAGNATRON BLVD., #A
SAN DIEGO CA 92111

MMV LLC
4221 Wilshire Blvd Suite 290-3
Los Angeles CA 90010

The Jackson Agency LLC
1901 Avenue of the Stars, Second Floor
Century City CA 90067

HOLLYWOOD TALENT
AGENCY DIRECTORY

WE ARE VOICES ENTERTAINMENT, INC.
9350 CIVIC CENTER DR.
BEVERLY HILLS CA 90210

Jemetra Trotter dba Peridot Talent Agency
44641 Alighchi Way
Temecula CA 92592

DIZON LLC
353 Sacramento Street, 18th Floor
San Francisco CA 94111

Edward Gradford dba emusicmanager
1202 H Street Ste C
Modesto CA 95354

CIRCLE TALENT AGENCY, LLC
5900 WILSHIRE BLVD., STE. 2200
LOS ANGELES CA 90036

Aaron Jordan dba SKILD
6522 Oakgrove Circle
Huntington Beach CA 92647

Stars Model Management
23 Grant Avenue, 4th Floor
San Francisco CA 94108

HOLLYWOOD TALENT
AGENCY DIRECTORY

S.I.INSTITUTE dba TEAM ONE TALENT
AGENCY
321 LARCHMONT BLVD.
LOS ANGELES CA 90004

SAN DIEGO MODEL MANAGEMENT TALENT
AGENCY
438 CAMINO DEL RIO S. #116
SAN DIEGO CA 92108

THE SARNOFF COMPANY, INC.
1600 ROSECRANS AVE., BLDG 1A, 2ND FLR,
STE 203-204
MANHATTAN BEACH CA 90266

MARY ELIZABETH DANGERFIELD dba
DANGERFIELD TALENT
13500 VENTURA BLVD.
SHERMAN OAKS CA 91423

Claudia Sobreira DiVito dba DUNA
PRODUCTIONS AND
9933 Wells Rd.
Malibu CA 90265

HOLLYWOOD TALENT
AGENCY DIRECTORY

SHORTLIST MODEL AND TALENT AGENCY,
LLC
100 SHORELINE HIGHWAY, BUILDING B,
SUITE 100
MILL VALLEY CA 94941

KIRA PULLEN dba UNLIMITED
POSSIBILITIES MUSIC & T
9350 MOONBEAM AVE., #5
PANORAMA CITY CA 91402

AMERICAN MODELS & ACTORS, LLC
2900 SOUTH HARBOR BLVD., #230
SANTA ANA CA 92704

25 LIVE, LLC
25 MUSIC SQUARE WEST
NASHVILLE TN 37203

SHINN ENTERTAINMENT CORPORATION
dba INTERNATIONAL
191 E CITY PLACE DR.
SANTA ANA CO 92705

THE LIONS MODEL MANAGEMENT LLC
9130 WEST SUNSET BLVD.
LOS ANGELES CA 90069

HOLLYWOOD TALENT
AGENCY DIRECTORY

BRAND MODEL & TALENT AGENCY, INC.
601 N. Baker Street
Santa Ana CA 92703

Annette Van Duren
3810 Wilshire Boulevard #1906
Los Angeles CA 90010   05/13/2020
The Library Agency, LLC
5900 Sepulveda Boulevard, #580
Sherman Oaks CA 91411

Lips LLC
6417 Selma Ave, 2nd Floor
Los Angeles CA 90028

PRINCIPAL ENTERTAINMENT LOS ANGELES
LLC
9255 W. SUNSET BLVD., #500
LOS ANGELES CA 90069

Rashon Velmont dba VELMONT TALENT
AGENCY
305 E 9th St., #300
Los Angeles CA 90015

DISRUPT THE GAME, LLC

HOLLYWOOD TALENT
AGENCY DIRECTORY

332 S. PECK DR.
BEVERLY HILLS CA 90212

PRODUCTIONS PLUS, INC. dba
PRODUCTIONS PLUS - THE
909 ELECTRIC AVE., STE. 204 & 205
SEAL BEACH CA 90740

MARTONE MGMT INC
3324 1/2 Bellevue Ave
Los Angeles CA 90026

Grace Marian Chan dba Grace Model
Management
12400 Ventura Blvd #421
Studio City CA 91401

Unbreakable Talent Inc.
1111 S. Victory Blvd., Ste. 252
Burbank CA 91502

MADAMOISELLE, INC. dba MADAMOISELLE
TALENT AGENCY
24328 VERMONT AVE., #309
HARBOR CITY CA 90710

BILL HOLLINGSHEAD PRODUCTIONS, INC.

HOLLYWOOD TALENT
AGENCY DIRECTORY

1010 ANDERSON RD.
DAVIS CA 95616

THOMAS H. CHASIN dba THOMAS CHASIN
AGENCY
8281 MELROSE AVE., #202
LOS ANGELES CA 90046

Northagenda llc dba quartz talent agency
8118 Irvine Ave
North Hollywood CA 91605

Ashley Marie Dalton dba Agency for Creative
Talen
1311 N Mansfield Ave A
Los Angeles CA 90028

THE HOLLRED AGENCY, INC.
5514 WILSHIRE BLVD., 1ST FLOOR
LOS ANGELES CA 90036

BELINDA A. IRONS dba SF TOP MODELS &
TALENT AGENCY
2261 MARKET STREET
SAN FRANCISCO CA 94114

DFA California, LLC dba The Dragonfly Agency

HOLLYWOOD TALENT
AGENCY DIRECTORY

6666 Lexington Avenue
Los Angeles CA 90038

IMG Models LA, LLC
700 N. San Vicente Blvd, Suite G-600, Sixth
Floor
Los Angeles CA 90069

KCW Consulting Group
1122 2nd Street
Hermosa Beach CA 90254

DECAYETTE TALENT AGENCY LLC
260 South Beverly Drive, Suite 205
Beverly Hills CA 90212

Tanya La Salle Caravelli dba La Salle Talent
26565 West Agoura Rd. Su. 200
Calabasas CA 91302

Mix Models, Inc.
2660 Townsgate Road Suite 400
Westlake Village CA 91361

Dalena T Hoang dba Model and Talent
Management
2200 Eastridge Loop, #1004-B
San Jose CA 95122

Limelight Talent, Inc.

HOLLYWOOD TALENT
AGENCY DIRECTORY

8149 SANTA MONICA BLVD., UNIT 287
LOS ANGELES CA 90046

Limelight Talent, Inc.
8149 SANTA MONICA BLVD., UNIT 287
LOS ANGELES CA 90046

Hyperion Talent Agency, LLC
8383 Wilshire Blvd., Suite 702
Beverly Hills CA 90211

SKAM ARTIST, INC.
1616 Vista Del Mar St
Los Angeles CA 90028

ROBERTSON/TAYLOR AGENCY LLC
11500 W. OLYMPIC BLVD., STE. 400
LOS ANGELES CA 90064

NANCY CHAIDEZ AGENCY & ASSOCIATES,
INC.
6340 COLDWATER CANYON AVE., UNIT 214
NORTH HOLLYWOOD CA 91606

AMT ARTISTS, INC.
15260 VENTURA BLVD., #1200
SHERMAN OAKS CA 91403

DAIRY A. VERAS REEVES dba UNIVERSAL
TALENT AGENCY

HOLLYWOOD TALENT
AGENCY DIRECTORY

4221 WILSHIRE BLVD., STE. 290-17
LOS ANGELES CA 90010

MICHAEL JAMES WALLACH dba MICHAEL
WALLACH MANAGEMENT
908 Granville Avenue, Suite 300
Los Angeles CA 90049

Panache Booking LLC
4516 1/2 Eagle Rock Blvd
Los Angeles CA 90041

JENNIFER POWELL, INC.
16000 Ventura Boulevard, #900
Encino CA 91436

THE VIP CONNECT, INC.
15206 VENTURA BLVD. #210
SHERMAN OAKS CA 91403

Prestigious Models Inc dba Image Powerhouse
Agency
11101 Condor Avenue
Fountain Valley CA 92708

Jessica Lange dba The Rosenstein Agency
5455 Wilshire Blvd. STE. 2020

HOLLYWOOD TALENT
AGENCY DIRECTORY

Los Angeles CA 90036

ACTIVITY, INC.
4705 LAUREL CANYON BLVD., STE. 203
STUDIO CITY CA 91607

TRITON TALENT AGENCY
11328 MAGNOLIA BLVD.
NORTH HOLLYWOOD CA 91601

THE SELLMAN GROUP, INC.
926 S. ORANGE GROVE AVE.
LOS ANGELES CA 90036

GWYN FOXX dba GFTA GWYN FOXX
TALENT AGENCY
2600 W. Olive Ave
BURBANK CA 91505

ASTERINO ENTERTAINMENT AGENCY, LLC
9595 Wilshire Boulevard 9th Floor
Beverly Hills CA 90212

Steven Tsepelis dba Steve Tsepelis
3619 E 1st St Apt #5
Long Beach CA 90803

Folklore Inc. a/k/a Fli Artists dba FLi Artists
11321 Iowa Avenue Suite#6

HOLLYWOOD TALENT AGENCY DIRECTORY

Los Angeles CA 90025

SOLID TALENT INC.
11012 Ventura Boulevard, Unit G
Studio City CA 91604

Ford Models, Inc.
11 E. 26th St., 14th Floor
New York NY 10010

Brown Family Enterprises LLC dba Power
Artists Ag
1901 Avenue of the Stars, Ste. 200
Century City CA 90067

United Talent Agency, LLC
9336-46 Civic Center Drive
Beverly Hills CA 90210

ROBERT EMMANUEL DEPPE dba Beverly
Hecht Agency
12100 WILSHIRE BLVD., SUITE 800
LOS ANGELES CA 90025

Ayinde Banjoko dba Blue Steel
515 13th Street
Modesto CA

INNOVATIVE ARTISTS COMEDY DIVISION
1505 10TH ST
SANTA MONICA CA 90401

HOLLYWOOD TALENT
AGENCY DIRECTORY

Closeup Models and Talent LLC
5455 Wilshire blvd, Suite 2020
Los Angeles CA 90036

World Premier Agency, LLC
1015 12th St. Suite 10
Modesto CA 95354

CREATIVE VENTURES AGENCY, LLC
520 South Sepulveda Boulevard, Suite 303
Los Angeles CA 90049

True Til Death
8320 Fountain Ave. Apt. C
West Hollywood CA 90069

BMG TALENT GROUP, INC.
5455 WILSHIRE BOULEVARD, SUITE 900
LOS ANGELES CA 90036

MOXIE MODEL AND TALENT, LLC
111 W. OCEAN BLVD., SUITE 400
LONG BEACH CA 90802

Tabitha Kit Johnson dba Kit International Talent
201 Riverside Ave #1
Roseville CA 95678

HOLLYWOOD TALENT
AGENCY DIRECTORY

NEWMARK MODELS, INC.
5700 Melrose Ave #201
Los Angeles CA 90038

Natural Talent, Inc.
20265 Ventura Blvd., #D
Woodland Hills CA 91364

Alive In Motion Incorporated dba Thrive Artists A
1601 North Gower Street
Los Angeles CA 90028

INNOVATIVE ARTISTS
1505 10th Street
Santa Monica CA 90401

ROBERT BEARD dba GALAXY
ENTERTAINMENT
8484 WILSHIRE BLVD., #515
BEVERLY HILLS CA 90211

Angel Howansky dba Eure Entertainment
Agency 40942 Rise Ct
Palmdale CA 93551

The Blackwell Files LLC
3178 17th Street, Studio 3
San Francisco CA 94110

HOLLYWOOD TALENT
AGENCY DIRECTORY

Marc Blake dba Domremy Talent
6112 E Lowe Avenue
Fresno CA 93727

Bachelor & Associates Consulting, LLC dba
Bach Ta
3800 Braham Blvd, Suite 315
Los Angeles CA 90068

If Management Inc
152 West 57th Street, Floor 19
New York NY 10019

Evolved Talent Agency LLC
1801 Century Park East, FL 25
Los Angeles CA 90067

Lisa Christensen dba The Livingston Agency
730 Arizona Ave.
Santa Monica CA 90401

Baron Entertainment, Inc.
13848 Ventura Blvd. Suite A
Sherman Oaks CA 91423

90210 TALENT, INC.
16430 VENTURA BLVD., STE. 200
ENCINO CA 91436

HOLLYWOOD TALENT
AGENCY DIRECTORY

Paddle Out People, LLC
13212 Anawood Way
Westminster CA 92683

HENDERSON REPRESENTS, INC.
11846 VENTURA BLVD.
STUDIO CITY CA 91604

Brandon Louis Management, LLC
915 N. La Brea Ave #641
West Hollywood CA 90038

Beth Bohn Management, Inc.
2420 Lake View Avenue
Los Angeles CA 90039

INNOVATIVE ARTISTS COMMERCIAL AND
VOICEOVER, INC.
1505 10TH ST
SANTA MONICA CA 90401

JAMES SPEARS
1800 CENTURY PARK EAST, STE. 1000
LOS ANGELES CA 90067

REFRESH TALENT AGENCY, INC.
24632 LA PLATA
LAGUNA NIGUEL CA 92677

HOLLYWOOD TALENT
AGENCY DIRECTORY

ATEI COMPANY, INC. dba TEI
ENTERTAINMENT dba THA
3820 E. LA PALMA AVENUE
ANAHEIM CA 92807

Blackboard Production, LLC
11848 Kiowa ave, apt PH6
Los Angeles CA 90049

Margaux Models LLC dba Margaux Models
210 Santa Monica Blvd. #306
Santa Monica CA 90401

The Talent Agancy, Inc.
7507 Sunset Blvd. Suite 201
Los Angeles CA 90046

Power Talent Group dba Power Talent Agency
13900 Marquesas Way Suite #5402
Marina Del Rey CA 90292

LACREA LLC
530 S Hewitt St Unit 155
Los Angeles CA 90013

PACIFIC TALENT & MODELS, INC.
1600 ROSECRANS AVE., MEDIA CENTER,
4TH FLOOR

HOLLYWOOD TALENT
AGENCY DIRECTORY

MANHATTAN BEACH CA 90266

CHRISTINE BERNARD dba ERIS TALENT
AGENCY
9595 WILSHIRE BLVD., SUITE 900
BEVERLY HILLS CA 90212

FLICK EAST & WEST TALENTS, INC.
9057 NEMO ST
WEST HOLLYWOOD CA 90069

SHAMON FREITAS & COMPANY, INC. dba
SHAMON FREITAS
3916 OREGON ST.
SAN DIEGO CA 92104

XCEL TALENT AGENCY LLC
3525 PIEDMONT ROAD NE BUILDING 7
SUITE 300
ATLANTA GA 30305

BBA Talent Inc.
3500 W. Olive Avenue Suite 300
Burbank CA 91505

Debbie Britt dba Cornerstone Talent
Management
16501 Ventura Blvd. Ste. 400
Encino CA 91436

HOLLYWOOD TALENT
AGENCY DIRECTORY

Andrea Barton dba STARLIGHT AGENCY
8484 Wilshire Blvd. #515
Beverly Hills CA 90211

Artists Management Agency, Inc.
738 S Ogden Drive #302
Los Angeles CA 90036

ALLIVE ENTERTAINMENT LLC dba ALLIVE
AGENCY
324 S. BEVERLY DR STE. 546
BEVERLY HILLS CA 90212

JACK LIPPMAN AGENCY, INC. dba JLA (JACK
LIPPMAN A
9151 SUNSET BLVD
WEST HOLLYWOOD CA 90069

The Acoustic Spot, LLC
640 Grand Ave. Suite G
Carlsbad CA 92008

Kira Pullen dba UNLIMITED POSSIBILITIES
MUSIC & T
9350 Moonbeam Ave Ste 5
Panorama City CA 91402

HOLLYWOOD TALENT
AGENCY DIRECTORY

CARISSA MITCHELL dba Mitchell & Associates
Talent
18356 OXNARD ST., #7
TARZANA CA 91356

YUKA ENTERPRISES, LLC
642 N. ROBERTSON BLVD.
WEST HOLLYWOOD CA 90069

AMERICAN MEDIA ARTISTS, INC.
4830 ENCINO AVE.
ENCINO CA 91316

YG Entertainment USA, Inc.
741 Crenshaw Blvd.
Los Angeles CA 90005

RSA Talent Management, LLC
1000 N. Reese Place
Burbank CA 91506

C Talent, LLC
1149 N. Gower St., Ste. 251B
Los Angeles CA 90038

HOLLYWOOD TALENT
AGENCY DIRECTORY

MELODY LOMBOY AND THOMAS E. LOWE
dba L & L Talent
655 Deep Valley Drive #325A
Rolling Hills Estates CA 90274

SPIN ARTIST AGENCY
8335 W SUNSET BLVD., STE. 200
LOS ANGELES CA 90069

ORGANIC TALENT, LLC
1016 Wilcox Avenue, #9
Los Angeles CA 90038

Electra Star Modeling Agency, LLC
9229 SUNSET BLVD, Suite 415,
West Hollywood CA 90069

B'NAI MARIE TALENT AGENCY
27240 Turnberry Lane, Suite 200
Valencia CA 91355

Vince Spadea dba Vince Models
100 N. Doheny Dr. Suite 104
Los Angeles CA 90048

SIX O'CLOCK STUDIOS, LLC
13636 Ventura Blvd #238
Sherman Oaks CA 91423

HOLLYWOOD TALENT
AGENCY DIRECTORY

Stephen D. Linett
1901 Avenue of the Stars, Suite 1100
Los Angeles CA 90067

Steven C. Bernier dba Street Dreams
Productions
3911 Harrison Street
Oakland CA 94611

Christopher Maggiore dba artists worldwide
3660 Wilshire blvd #1134
Los Angeles CA 90010

Shauntiel Lindsey dba Shauntiel Lindsey Talent
8484 Wilshire Blvd Suite 515
Beverly Hills CA 90210

Green and Green Talent Group
6363 Wilshire Boulevard, Apt. 400
Los Angeles CA 90048

Michael Richard Lewis dba Michael Lewis &
Associa
2506 Fifth Street, Suite 100
Santa Monica CA 90405

Actors and Artists Agency LLC
16911 Devonshire Street
Granada Hills CA 91344

HOLLYWOOD TALENT
AGENCY DIRECTORY

Beotis Creative LLC
8950 W Olympic Blvd, STE 293
Beverly Hills CA 90211

National Models LA LLC dba National Talent LA
22809 Pacific Coast Highway Suite 210
Malibu CA 90265

Christine Bernard dba Eris Talent Agency
9595 Wilshire Blvd. Suite 900
Beverly Hills CA 90212

CIRCLE TALENT AGENCY, LLC
5900 WILSHIRE BLVD, SUITE 2200
LOS ANGELES CA 90036

Howard L. Sapper dba Extrordinaire Media
752 Broadway
Sonoma CA 95476

David Davinci
5000 Birch Street, West Tower, Suite 3000
Newport Beach CA 92660

Eleven Talent Agency, Inc.
121 West Lexington Drive, Suite 258
Glendale CA 91203

HOLLYWOOD TALENT
AGENCY DIRECTORY

Models Inc Talent Agency
264 Spring St.
Pleasanton CA 94566

The Jumbo Shrimp Circus,, Inc
20315 Baltar St
Winnetka CA 91306

Kevin Brent Harvey dba Hollywood Music in
Media A
7646 Kester Avenue
Van Nuys CA 91405

Sheneka Majors dba Major Multimedia
501 W. Broadway Suite 800, 8th Floor
San Diego CA 92101

The Haole LLC dba Trinity Artists International
1901 Avenue of The Stars #202
Los Angeles CA 90067

Nomad Management Los Angeles, LLC
8430 Santa Monica Boulevard, Suite 204
West Hollywood CA 90069

LIAISON ARTISTS LLC
2343 3rd Street #299
San Francisco CA 94107

HOLLYWOOD TALENT
AGENCY DIRECTORY

310 Artists Agency
3500 W Olive Ave #300
Burbank CA 91505

King's Queens Entertainment
858 Westbourne Dr #8
West Hollywood CA 90069

Melody Mcclendon dba Stylish Confessions
Modeling
27240 Turnberry lane
Valencia CA 91355

Alchemy By Faust, LLC
1375 Cole Road
Aromas CA 95004

Tiffany Richer dba RPM Talent
2600 W.Olive Ave., 5th Floor
Burbank CA 91505

MURTHA SKOURAS AGENCY
1025 COLORADO AVE., Suite B
SANTA MONICA CA 90401

SAINT AGENCY INC
925 N. La Brea Ave,, 4th floor
Los Angeles CA 90038

HOLLYWOOD TALENT
AGENCY DIRECTORY

Boudoir Agency, LLC.
1600 Rosecrans Ave. Media Center 4th Floor
Manhattan Beach CA 90266

Get Heavy Talent Agency & Events LLC
26072 Merit Circle #115
Laguna Hills CA 92653

CINDY ROMANO MODELING & TALENT
AGENCY   73-101 Highway 111, #7
Palm Desert CA 92260

Affinity Models & Talent, Inc. dba Affinity Artis
5455 Wilshire Blvd #1010
Los Angeles CA 90036

David Shapira & Associates Inc.
193 N. Robertson Blvd
Beverly Hils CA 90211

Ikais Entertainment
4085 West 138th Street Apt C
Hawthorne CA 90250

Lynn Nicholson dba Top Rock Entertainment
4811 Cathy Avenue
Cypress CA 90630

HOLLYWOOD TALENT
AGENCY DIRECTORY

Top Rock Entertainment
4811 Cathy Avenue
Cypress CA 90630

Aqua, LLC
9000 Sunset Blvd.,Suite 700
West Hollywood CA 90069

LUXE TALENT AGENCY, INC
1320 5th Avenue, Suite 3B
San Diego CA 92101

Commercial Talent, Inc
12711 Ventura Blvd. Ste# 285
Studio City CA 91604   03/

David Victor Presents LLC
1551 Asterbell Dr
San Ramon CA   94582

SMC PARTNERS, INC.
3477 Maricopa Street, Suite 17
Torrance CA 90503

Executive PR and Talent, LLC dba The
Benedetti Gr
1916 Bechelli Lane
Redding CA 96002

HOLLYWOOD TALENT
AGENCY DIRECTORY

Michael Dean Wagner dba The Wagner Agency
956 W 8th Street
San Pedro CA 90731

VERVE TALENT & LITERARY AGENCY, LLC
6310 San Vicente Blvd, Ste 100
Los Angeles CA 90048

Resolute Talent Group, Inc.
1601 Vine Street 6th Floor
Los Angeles CA 90028

BEST-Napoli Group, LLC dba NAPOLI
MANAGEMENT GROU
8844 W. Olympic Boulevard, Suite 100
Beverly Hills CA 90211

Role Models Management LLC
701 West Manchester Blvd #203
Inglewood CA 90301

PUREFLARE LLC
655 North Central Avenue, 17th Floor
Glendale CA 91203

Artery Global LLC
7200 Fair Oaks Blvd #230
Carmichael CA 95608

HOLLYWOOD TALENT
AGENCY DIRECTORY

MARI SMITH PRESENTS INC. dba MARI
SMITH PRESENTS,
101 State Place - Suite D
Escondido CA 92029

Thrive Entertainment LLC
8605 West Santa Monica Blvd #19407
West Hollywood CA 90069

Goldenchild International LLC
117 S. Doheny Drive #209
Beverly Hills CA 90048

ORIGINAL ARTISTS
2801 Hyperion Avenue, Studio 104
Los Angeles CA 90027

MDT Talent Agency, Inc. dba Marla Dell Talent
Age
2124 Union Street, Suite C
San Francisco CA 94123

Eris Talent Agency, Inc.
15303 Ventura Boulevard, Suite 900
Sherman Oaks CA 91403

Eye for Talent, Inc.
751 Laurel Street, #113
San Carlos CA 94070

HOLLYWOOD TALENT
AGENCY DIRECTORY

JUAN DUARTE AVRAVANEL BERDUGO dba
Abravanel Talen
1322 S. Gerhart Ave
Commerce CA 90022

High Voltage Entertainment, Inc. dba Project
Taku
3019 Pico Blvd, Ste 5
Santa Monica CA 90405

GIANNELLI ENTERTAINMENT, LLC
1201 West 5th Street, Suite F180
Los Angeles CA 90017

Claudia Sobreira DiVito dba Duna Productions
9933 Yerba Buena Road
Malibu CA 90265

Spin Artist Agency
8335 W Sunset Blvd# 200
Los Angeles CA 90069

Iconic Talent Agency
1925 Century Park East, 17th Floor Office #38
Los Angeles CA 90067

MARTIN HALLEN & DANIELA M. WULFF dba
PTI Talent
275 East Hillcrest Drive, Suite 160-215
Thousand Oaks CA 91360

HOLLYWOOD TALENT
AGENCY DIRECTORY

Ideal Talent Agency LLC
10806 Ventura Boulevard, #2
Studio City CA 91604

LUNA MANAGEMENT LLC
1200 Venice Boulevard
Los Angeles CA 90006

Eventos, Inc.
15058 Killion Street
Sherman Oaks CA 91411

Var-E Music LLC dba NT Talent Agency
360 Banbridge Avenue
La Puente CA 91744

PENNY MARIE STUBBS dba MPM Models
29983 Loy Drive
Menifee CA 92585

The Finest Model Talent LLC
24631 Mendocino Ct.
Laguna Hills CA 92653

Sheila Groves - Tracey
2915 Lake Redding Drive
Redding, CA 96003

CLINTON GUNNELS dba Fame Talent Agency

HOLLYWOOD TALENT
AGENCY DIRECTORY

1441 N. McCadden Place
Los Angeles CA 90028

BOUNTY LA LLC
1601 Vine Street
Los Angeles CA 90028

Ronald O'Hannon and Jyvonne Haskin dba
GREYLOC AG
714 S Los Angeles St. Unit 507
Los Angeles CA 90014

Earth to Peter LLC
10547 National Blvd. #3
Los Angeles CA 90034

Genius Enterprises, LLC
5318 W 64th St
Inglewood CA 90302

33 and West LLC
309 East 8th Street, Suite 603
Los Angeles CA 90014

Metric Models LLC
11901 Goshen Avenue, #305
Los Angeles CA 90049

Ambition Modeling and Talent Agency

HOLLYWOOD TALENT
AGENCY DIRECTORY

3425 Wilson Avenue, #1
Oakland CA 94602

THE MILTON AGENCY, INC.
6715 Hollywood Boulevard, #206
Los Angeles CA 90028

REPUBLIC NETWORK INC.
993 C. S. Santa Fe Ave #245
Vista CA 92083

DAIRY A. VERAS REEVES dba UNIVERSAL
TALENT AGENCY
4221 Wilshire Boulevard, Suite 290-17
Los Angeles CA 90010

Line by Line, LLC
12130 Millennium Drive, Suite 300
Los Angeles CA 90094

Ali Delaram dba Electra Star Talent Agency
9229 West Sunset Blvd, 415
West Hollywood CA 90069

THE CRITERION GROUP, INC. dba Criterion
Group
4842 Sylmar Avenue
Sherman Oaks CA 91423

STATE ARTIST MANAGEMENT LLC

HOLLYWOOD TALENT
AGENCY DIRECTORY

8075 W. 3rd Street, #307
Los Angeles CA 90048

TANGERINE TALENT, LLC
5250 Lankershim Boulevard, Suite 500
North Hollywood CA 91601-3187

Envy Model & Talent LLC
489 S. Robertson Boulevard, #104A
Beverly Hills CA 90211

Theodis Wiley dba Making Stars Talent Agency
509 E. Bella Terrace
Bakersfield CA 93307

HOLLANDER TALENT GROUP, INC.
14011 Ventura Boulevard, Suite 202
Sherman Oaks CA 91423

Wild Wolves Talent Agency LLC
6250 Canoga Ave #385
Woodland Hills CA 91367

AIM ARTISTS AGENCY, LLC
10846 Baird Avenue
Northridge CA 91326

Jeenyus Entertainment
1010 N. Central Avenue, Suite 313

HOLLYWOOD TALENT
AGENCY DIRECTORY

Glendale CA 91202

Ivy Lundeen
23401 Winslow Place
Valencia CA 91354

Belinda A. Irons dba SF Top Models & Talent
Agency
2261 Market Street, #295
San Francisco CA 94114

Gold Standard Sports & Entertainment
2447 PCH, Ste 200
Hermosa Beach CA 90254

JOE KOLKOWITZ dba PLAYERS TALENT
AGENCY
16130 Ventura Boulevard, suite 235
Encino CA 91436

Todd J Stein dba Stein Entertainment Group
3900 W. Alameda Ave., #1200
Burbank CA 91505

Unbound Artists, LLC
1731 15th Street #309
San Francisco CA 94103

NB Creative, LLC dba District Model and Talent
1902 Wright Place 2nd floor

HOLLYWOOD TALENT
AGENCY DIRECTORY

Carlsbad, CA 92008

Business Management LAB, Inc
279 Downs Rd
Tustin CA 92782

Dennis D. Strazulo dba Marin Artist
Management
1010 B Street, Suite 300
San Rafael CA 94901

MAGDALENA TALENT, INC. dba MAGDALENA
TALENT/MAGDA
1600 Rosecrans Ave., 4th Floor
Manhattan Beach CA 90266

3 ARTIST MANAGEMENT INC.
12100 WILSHIRE BL STE 1540
LOS ANGELES CA 90025

ELLIS TALENT GROUP
4705 Laurel Canyon Boulevard, Suite 300
Valley Village CA 91607

Christina Aude dba STAR TOUCH AGENCY
1545 Wilcox Ave Ste 201
Los Angeles CA 90028

Seven Stars Talent Inc.
6320 Canoga Avenue, Suite 1500

Woodland Hills CA 91367

TROY BRONSTEIN dba T-BEST TALENT
AGENCY
3544 ARDEN RD
HAYWARD CA 94545

MemBrain, LLC
1800 Century Park East, Suite 1000
Los Angeles CA 90067

BIG MONEY BRANDI MANAGEMENT, INC.
dba BMB Talent
28720 Roardside Dr. STE 354
Agoura Hills CA 91301

DFA California, LLC dba The Dragonfly Agency
1855 Industrial St. #111A
Los Angeles CA 90021

Kirkland Productions, Inc.
6711 Katella Avenue, 2nd Floor
Cypress CA 90630

Kirkland Productions, Inc.
6711 Katella Avenue, 2nd Floor
Cypress CA 90630

Baron Entertainment Group, Inc.
13848 Ventura Blvd. Suite A

HOLLYWOOD TALENT
AGENCY DIRECTORY

Sherman Oaks CA 91423

ALEX MOREHOUSE dba MORE TALENT 555
w 5th Street
Los Angeles CA 90014

D/R Welch Attorneys at Law A Professional
Corporat
500 South Grand Avenue Suite 1800
Los Angeles CA 90071

Talent Branded Entertainment, Inc.
2445 North Naomi Street
Burbank CA 91504

DIVISION WEST MANAGEMENT, LLC dba
Frank Model Management
5600 Avenida Encinas, Suite 140A
Carlsbad CA 92008

MARILYN WILCHER dba THE DAWSON
AGENCY
1660 N. Wilton Place, Suite 411
Los Angeles CA 90028

MARTA DAVIS dba HOLLYWOOD-
VANCOUVER-NEW YORK TALE

HOLLYWOOD TALENT
AGENCY DIRECTORY

1010 Wilshire Boulevard
Los Angeles CA 90017

Williams Entertainment Group LLC dba Impact
Talen
21151 S. Western Ave
Torrance CA 90501

Public Figures Agency LLC
7323 Winnetka Ave., Apt. 112
Winnetka CA 91306

Luxe Fit Inc. dba Luxe Fit Models
9415 Culver Blvd.
Culver City CA 90232

Professionally Pretty Inc.
1303 W. Fairbanks Ave
Winter Park FL 32789

Neer Motion, LLC
6525 W. Sunset Blvd., Suite G1/Mailbox 4
Los Angeles CA 90028

Adam Sinjin Park dba Park Noack Agency
10866 Wilshire Boulevard, Suite 400
Los Angeles CA 90024

HOLLYWOOD TALENT
AGENCY DIRECTORY

Sound Talent Group LLC
6156 Camino Largo
SAN DIEGO CA 92120-3115

Allen J Williamson Jr. dba Big Yellow Door
Talent
10975 Bluffside Dr, #1125
Studio City CA 91604

Abrams Artists Agency, LLC
750 N. San Vicente Blvd., East Tower, 11th
Floor
Los Angeles CA 90069

TAYLOR TALENT SERVICES INC.
4859 Katherine Avenue
Sherman Oaks CA 91423

White Cross Productions INC dba White Cross
Manag
26500 Agoura Road #525
Calabasas CA 91302

The NWT Group, LLC
2325 Stonebridge Drive
Arlington TX 76006

HOLLYWOOD TALENT
AGENCY DIRECTORY

About Entertainment LLC
1207 West Magnolia Boulevard, Suite D
Burbank CA 91506

Panagiotis Kallinteris dba Peter Kallinteris Agen
1438 N. Gower Street, Bldg. 2, Room 39 - Box
87
Los Angeles CA 90028

KOD MUSIC, LLC
413 N BRAND BLVD UNIT 110
GLENDALE CA 91203

CAMILLE SORICE dba Camille Sorice Agency
11715 Hortense Street
Valley Village CA 91607

247 Casting Call
6060 COLFAX AVE, APT 3
NORTH HOLLYWOOD CA 91606

Olivia Andrade Talent Agency
2048 E Ave R10
Palmdale CA 93550

Flappers Comedy LLC DBA H2F Comedy
Productions db
102 E. Magnolia Blvd.
Burbank CA 91502

HOLLYWOOD TALENT
AGENCY DIRECTORY

JOAQUIN SAHAGUN dba AVAIL TALENT LA
12501 Philadelphia St. #109
Whittier CA 90601

The Park View Agency LLC
925 La Brea Ave
Los Angeles CA 90038

CLINTON GUNNELS dba Fame Talent Agency
1441 North McCadden Place
Los Angeles CA 90028

Royalty Business Solutions
15481 Tobarra Rd
Fontana CA 92337

Actor's Alliance Group, LLC
15514 S Western Ave #C
Gardena CA 90249

GWYN FOXX dba GFTA Gwyn Foxx Talent
Agency
2600 W. OLIVE AVE.
BURBANK CA 91505

Osbrink Talent Agency Inc.
2222 W Olive Avenue
Burbank CA 91506

HOLLYWOOD TALENT
AGENCY DIRECTORY

Diamond M Gail dba Makena's Talent Agency
4500 Park Granada Blvd. Suite 202
Calabasas CA 91302

NEER MOTION, LLC
6525 W. Sunset Boulevard, Suite G1
Los Angeles CA 90028

BLACK ENTOURAGE TALENT MANAGEMENT
LLC
9800 Sepulveda Boulevard, #22
North Hills CA 91343

Christopher Dale McGrew dba HydeOut Talent
Agency
1546 Pershing Dr. Apt. A
San Francisco CA 94129

Kathy Marie Clewell dba WEF TALENT
AGENCY
15525 Pomerado Rd A4
Poway CA 92064

Halamay Entertainment LLC
20 S. Santa Cruz Avenue, Suite 300
Los Gatos CA 95030

Influencer Ventures, LLC

HOLLYWOOD TALENT
AGENCY DIRECTORY

28422 Constellation Rd #204
Santa Clarita CA 91355

Meridian Agency International dba SUMMIT
TALENT &
9454 Wilshire Blvd. Suite 203
Beverly Hills CA 90212

Sauers Media Group, LLC
13212 Anawood Way
Westminster CA 92683

Forefront Talent LLC
4654 7th Street
Carpinteria CA 93013

Paul Vertsekha and Scott Stewart Roush dba
LUBOVE
511 E. Gutierrez St. Ste.A
Santa Barbara CA 93103

Firestarter Entertainment, LLC dba Firestarter
En
21550 Oxnard Street, Suite 300
Woodland Hills CA 91367

EVOLVE ARTISTS AGENCY LLC

HOLLYWOOD TALENT
AGENCY DIRECTORY

3900 W Alameda Ave
Burbank CA 91505

Stephen Belafonte
7095 Hollywood Blvd., #576
Los Angeles CA 90028

MARTIN HALLEN & DANIELA M. WULFF dba
PTI Talent
275 EAST HILLCREST DR., #160-215
THOUSAND OAKS CA 91360

Florence Fischer Agency LLC
8560 W. Sunset Blvd 5th floor, #522
West Hollywood CA 90069

Meraki Management, Inc.
953 Cole Avenue
Los Angeles CA 90038

John T. Paizis dba 98 West Talent
231 E. Spruce Avenue
Inglewood CA 90301

A LIST AGENCY LLC
530 W Knoll Dr. # E
LOS ANGELES CA 90048

The Social Media Agency, Inc.
1556 20th Street, Unit D
Santa Monica CA 90404

HOLLYWOOD TALENT
AGENCY DIRECTORY

Alison Scholtz dba Leftside Talent Management
1020 North Normandie Ave
Los Angeles CA 90029

Young Hollywood Talent, LLC
10531 4S Commons Dr Suite 418
San Diego CA 92127

BONITA ELLEN HART dba Avenue Actors
Agency
12435 Oxnard Street
North Hollywood CA 91606

SIDNEY JAY LEVIN dba THE LEVIN AGENCY
8484 Wilshire Boulevard, Suite 750
Beverly Hills CA 90211

BARBARA BITELA
6228 Summerset Lane
Citrus Heights CA 95621

Robert Alexander Drieslein dba Uncle Snoops
Army
9950 Bellranch Dr Ste. 104
Santa Fe Springs CA 90670

REGINA CLENETTE MANAGEMENT, LLC
1232 Burnett Street

HOLLYWOOD TALENT
AGENCY DIRECTORY

Berkeley CA 94702

Terishka Elizabeth Franco dba V Agency L.A.
633 West 5th Street #2686
Los Angeles CA 90013

Hayes Talent Agency
10100 Santa Monica Blvd. STE 300
Los Angeles CA 90067

3506 Entertainment Inc. dba ACROSS THE
BOARD TALE
14542 Ventura Blvd, Suite 201
Sherman Oaks CA 914030

Lita D. Schloss aka Leigh Castle dba Castle Hill
1101 South Orlando Avenue
Los Angeles CA 90035

Gold Mind Agency LLC
5757 West Century Blvd, Suite 700
LOS ANGELES CA 90045

MICHAEL LIVINGSTON & JAMES R. COTA
dba THE ARTIST
9430 Olympic Boulevard, Suite 400
Beverly Hills CA 90212

Silverfox Management Group Inc.
1617 Cosmo Street, Suite 113

HOLLYWOOD TALENT
AGENCY DIRECTORY

Los Angeles CA 90028

Storm Management LLC
8797 Beverly Boulevard, Suite 304
Los Angeles CA 90048

American Artists Group Talent Agency LLC
13321 Ventura Blvd, Suite C-2
Sherman Oaks CA 91423

Sheila Groves - Tracey dba Notable Talent
2915 Lake Redding Dr.
Redding CA 96003

3D Public Relations and Marketing, Inc. dba 3d
Co
6340 Coldwater Canyon Ave. Ste. 206
North Hollywood CA 91606

Luke Johnstone dba Dig-It Talent
77 Shotwell Street, Unit 3
San Francisco CA 94103

TWICE BAKED MEDIA, INC. dba MOTLEY
MODELS
5636 Blanco Avenue
Woodland CA 91367

PHOTOGENICS MEDIA LLC
3103A S. LA CIENEGA BLVD

HOLLYWOOD TALENT
AGENCY DIRECTORY

LOS ANGELES CA 90016

Music Zirconia Talent LLC
5595 Magnatron Boulevard, #A
San Diego CA 92111

SHANNON MICHELLE LOAR-COTE dba
HELLO GORGEOUS MOD
27 East Victoria, Suite N
Santa Barbara CA 93101

FLO & ALLAN TALENT AGENCY LLC
1081 Long Beach Blvd. Apt. 114
Long Beach CA 90813

Faceroll, LLC
8383 Wilshire Blvd ste. 660
Beverly Hills CA 90211

The Empire Agency LLC
333 E 102nd St, #407
New York NY 10029

Laury Lee Smith dba Artists Among Us
7080 Hollywood Blvd. PH Level
Hollywood CA 90028

Cynthia Young Barry & Sandra Yvonne Hunter
dba Fi
13440 Ventura Boulevard, #211

HOLLYWOOD TALENT
AGENCY DIRECTORY

Sherman Oaks CA 91423

Shushu Entertainment, LLC
5805 White Oak Ave Unit 19277
Encino CA 91416

AMD VENTURES LLC dba CELESTINE
TALENT AGENCY
7250 Melrose Avenue, Suite 6
Los Angeles CA 90046

Embrace Real Artists LLC
15300 Ventura Blvd., Ste. 315
Sherman Oaks CA 91403

BEST Broadcasting & Media Talent, LLC dba 3
Kings
804 23rd Street
Manhattan Beach CA 90266

Henry Hoang
3050 West Ball rd spc 120
Anaheim CA 92804

David Victor Presents LLC
1551 Asterbell Drive
San Ramon CA 94582

HOLLYWOOD TALENT
AGENCY DIRECTORY

ALL AMERICAN RASCALS TALENT AGENCY
3349 Park Ridge Avenue
Bullhead City AZ 86429

Claudia Sobreira DiVito dba DUNA
PRODUCTIONS
9933 Yerba Buena Road
Malibu CA 90265

Miralee Menzies dba Miralee Menzies Talent
Agency
1644 1/2 Lucretia Ave.
Los Angeles CA 90026

ESSENTIAL ARTIST GROUP AGENCY, LLC
dba Connect En
22231 MULHOLLAND HWY, Ste. 112a
Calabasas CA 91302

Flower Power International LLC
5033 MacFarlane Lane
Woodland Hills CA 91364
TAMBELLINI PRODUCTIONS, INC. dba The
Event Consul
188 E. 17th St., Suite 201
Costa Mesa CA 92627

Erica Pierret dba Day7 Talent Agency

HOLLYWOOD TALENT
AGENCY DIRECTORY

7083 Hollywood Boulevard
Los Angeles CA 90028

Herold Model Management, LLC
29 Meadow Haven Lane
East Northport NY 11731

THE SELLMAN GROUP, INC.
926 S. ORANGE GROVE AVE.
LOS ANGELES CA 90036

Our Wave Model Management LLC
440 Upas Street #301
San Diego CA 92103

MARI SMITH PRESENTS, INC.
101 State Place, Suite D
Escondido CA 92029

Purple Oak Group Inc
925 N La Brea Ave, 4th Flr
Los Angeles CA 90038

U Model & Talent LLC dba UMT
1000 5th Street Suite 200-J6
Miami Beach FL 33139

THE HOWARD ROSE AGENCY, LTD.
9460 WILSHIRE BLVD., SUITE 310
BEVERLY HILLS CA 90210

HOLLYWOOD TALENT
AGENCY DIRECTORY

Iconic Talent Agency
1925 Century Park E, 17th Floor
Los Angeles CA 90067

EARTH TO PETER, LLC
10547 National Blvd. #3
Los Angeles CA 90034

Brand Model & Talent Agency, Inc.
601 N. Baker Street
Santa Ana CA 92703

Jackson Entertainment, LLC
1006 E. Olive
Burbank CA 91501

Wordsmith Literary Agency
29751 Strawberry Hill Dr.
Agoura Hills CA 91301

Bagula Riviere Coates and Associates, LLP
9888 Carroll Centre Road, #235
San Diego CA 92126

MPM MODELS, INC. dba MPM Models and
Talent Inc.
860 S. Los Angeles Street, Suite 704

HOLLYWOOD TALENT
AGENCY DIRECTORY

Los Angeles CA 90014

Tangerine Talent, LLC
5250 Lankershim Boulevard, Suite 500
North Hollywood CA 91601-3187

MUSE FIT MODELS INC.
12575 Beatrice Street
Los Angeles CA 90066

Mike Gatto
5419 Hollywood Boulevard Suite C-356
Los Angeles CA 90027

EXCEPTIONAL ARTISTS, LLC
4441 Forman Ave
Toluca Lake CA 91602

Dynamic Artists Management, LLC
5221 Central Avenue, Suite 202
Richmond CA 94804

KIANA PARKER dba VEYN TALENT
10999 Riverside Dr
North Hollywood CA 91602

Meriden Weems dba The Wanderlust
Experience
106 1/2 Judge John Aiso Street, #262

HOLLYWOOD TALENT
AGENCY DIRECTORY

Los Angeles CA 90012

DAVID EISENBERG dba PROTEGE
ENTERTAINMENT
710 E. ANGELENO AVENUE
BURBANK CA 91501

Billboard Artists Agency Inc.
4370 Tujunga Avenue, Suite 130
Studio City CA 91604

NICHOLAS A MORILLO dba CONTRA
AGENCY
236 N. CHESTER AVE
PASADENA CA 91106

Charles Lilly III
11950 Idaho Ave, #320
Los Angeles CA 90025

Encompass Talent, LLC
925 N. La Brea Ave. 4th Floor
Los Angeles CA 90038

Judith Fontaine Ellis dba FONTAINE-HERO
MODEL AND
12121 Wilshire Boulevard, Suite 203

HOLLYWOOD TALENT
AGENCY DIRECTORY

Los Angeles CA 90025

Wild Wolves Talent Agency LLC
6320 Canoga Avenue, 15th Floor
Woodland Hills CA 91367

KAZARIAN/MEASURES/RUSKIN &
ASSOCIATES, INC.
5200 Lankershim Boulevard, Suite 820
North Hollywood CA 91601

Above and Below The Surface LLC
1212H El Camino Real #231
San Bruno CA 94066

JEFFREY L DONOVAN
2154 Hercules Drive
Los Angeles CA 90046

Culture Creative Entertainment
15060 Ventura Blvd., Ste. 380
Sherman Oaks CA 91403

KIM CUNNINGHAM dba MALIBU ARTISTS
AGENCY
23733 Malibu Road, Suite 500
Malibu CA 90265

A4 AMELI ARTISTS AND ATHLETES
AGENCY, INC.
9171 Wilshire Boulevard, Suite 380

HOLLYWOOD TALENT
AGENCY DIRECTORY

Beverly Hills CA 90210

ABSTRACT TALENT, INC.
7119 Gerald Avenue
Van Nuys CA 91406

NANCY CHAIDEZ AGENCY & ASSOCIATES,
INC.
1800 N. Vine Street
Los Angeles CA 90028

JOHN E. HUTCHESON dba BOOM! MODELS
AND TALENT
2339 3rd Street, Suite, #47
San Francisco CA 94107

Artists Among Us Talent Agency LLC
1901 Ave of the Stars Suite 235
Los Angeles CA 90067

ALLEGRO TALENT GROUP, LLC
3445 Ridgeford Drive
Westlake Village CA 91361

Independent Artist Management, LLC dba
Independen
1800 North Vine Street
Hollywood CA 90028

HOLLYWOOD TALENT
AGENCY DIRECTORY

Feral Forever Inc. dba Sloane Models
981 Quarterhorse Lane
Oak Park CA 91377

Bad Moon Talent, LLC
731 N. Croft Ave.
Los Angeles CA 90069

Arnay LLC dba Arnay Talent Agency
6600 Lexington Ave #108
Hollywood CA 90038

LIKE MINDED MANAGEMENT LLC
17419 Burma Street
Encino CA 91316

Stephen Belafonte
7095 Hollywood Boulevard, #576
Los Angeles CA 90028

Quartz Talent Agency, LLC
665 Clela Avenue
East Los Angeles CA 90022

THREESIXTY SOCIETY LLC
889 Francisco Street Unit 2108
Los Angeles CA 90017

67 Ventures, Inc.

HOLLYWOOD TALENT
AGENCY DIRECTORY

649 Mission Street
San Francisco CA 94105

PHOTOGENICS TALENT LLC
3103A S. La Cienega Boulevard
Los Angeles CA 90016

CMG Worldwide, Inc.
9229 Sunset Boulevard, Suite 950
West Hollywood CA 90069

Stephen Leung dba So Cal Talent
16882 Bolsa Chica Street, Suite 108
Huntington Beach CA 92649

Dramatic Artists Agency, LA LLC
103 W. Alameda Avenue, Suite 139
Burbank CA 91502

ESPRIT TALENT AGENCY
11620 Wilshire Boulevard, 9th Floor
Los Angeles CA 90025

Green Light Talent Agency, Inc.
2811 Wilshire Blvd. Suite 570
Santa Monica CA 90403

West Artists Agency LLC

HOLLYWOOD TALENT
AGENCY DIRECTORY

8856 Warren Vista Ave
Yucca Valley CA 92284

Patricia Rile dba Patricia Rile Talent Agency
73 Pixy Place
Santa Rosa CA 95409

PLASTIC LLC
2069 Coldwater Canyon Drive
Beverly Hills CA 90210

Select Los Angeles, LLC
7250 Melrose Avenue Suite 4
Los Angeles CA 90046

Angelique Yalda
72740 Eagle Rd. #2
Palm Desert CA 92260

NEW DEAL MFG. CO
6363 Wilshire Blvd., Ste. 650
Los Angeles CA 90048

Scott Friedman
5849 La Cumbre Road
Somis CA 93066-9719

Troy Lawton dba Forge Ahead Touring

HOLLYWOOD TALENT
AGENCY DIRECTORY

2221 Bellevue Ave, Apt. 322
Los Angeles CA 90026

BYSB Talent LLC
1720 Peachtree Street, NW, #915
Atlanta GA 30309

EM ARTISTS LLC
7080 HOLLYWOOD BLVD., PH
Los Angeles CA 90028

5MC TALENT INC
1006 Voyager Drive
Bismarck ND 58504

CARLY CHRISTINE BIRKER
4322 Rhodes Avenue
Studio City CA 91604

Genuine Sports Group, LLC
111 Maiden Lane, 6th Floor
San Francisco CA 94108

HOLLYWOOD TALENT
AGENCY DIRECTORY

What you should have:

1. Headshot photograph taken by a professional photographer.

2. Acting/Model Resume with your past acting experience as well as your acting education. Cab be printed on the back of your Headshot or it can be stapled to the back of your Headshot.

3. Cover Sheet with a short introduction to get the attention of the Talent Agent you're contacting.

4. Education in Acting or Modeling. Take interest in learning more and honing your craft. You can do this by a combination of taking acting classes, reading acting books, attending plays, rehearsing lines from a script, and attending bookstores like Samuel French,

5. Positive Attitude is essential to progressing in your career. Believe in yourself and maintain an upbeat positive attitude.

Notes

HOLLYWOOD TALENT AGENCY DIRECTORY

Notes

HOLLYWOOD TALENT AGENCY DIRECTORY

MIKAZUKI PUBLISHING HOUSE™
(U.S.P.T.O. Serial Number 85705702)
1) 25 Principles of Martial Arts
2) 25 Principles of Strategy
3) American Antifa
4) American Bookstore Directory
5) Arctic Black Gold
6) Art of War
7) Back to Gold
8) Basketball Team Play Design Book
9) Beginner's Magicians Manual
10) Boxing Coloring Book
11) California's Next Century 2.0
12) Camping Survival Handbook
12) Captain Bligh's Voyage
13) Coming to America Handbook
14) Customer Sales Organizer

HOLLYWOOD TALENT AGENCY DIRECTORY

HOLLYWOOD TALENT
AGENCY DIRECTORY

42) Mythology Dictionary
43) Native Americana
44) Ninja Style
45) Ouija Board Enigma
46) Palloncino
47) Political Advertising Manual
48) Quotes Gone Wild
49) Rappers Rhyme Book
50) Saving America
51) Self-Examination Diary
52) Shinzen Karate
53) Shogun X the Last Immortal
54) Small Arms & Deep Pockets
55) Stories of a Street Performer
56) Storyboard Book
57) Swords & Sails
58) Tao Te Ching
59) The Adventures of Sherlock Holmes
60) The Art of Western Boxing
61) The Book of Five Rings
62) The Bribe Vibe
63) The Card Party
64) The History of Acid Tripping
65) The Man That Made the English Language
66) Tokiwa
67) T-Shirt Design Book
68) U.S. Army Anti-Guerrilla Warfare
    Manual
69) United Nations Charter
70) U.S. Military Boxing Manual
71) Van Carlton Detective Agency; The
    Burgundy Diamond

HOLLYWOOD TALENT
AGENCY DIRECTORY

72) William Shakespeare's Sonnets
73) Words of King Darius
74) World War Water
Facebook.com/MikazukiPublishingHouse

KAMBIZ MOSTOFIZADEH TITLES
1. 25 Principles of Martial Arts
2. 25 Principles of Strategy
3. American Antifa
4. American Bookstore Directory
5. Arctic Black Gold
6. Back To Gold
7. Camping Survival Handbook
8. Economic Collapse Survival Manual
9. Find the Ideal Husband
10. Game Creation Manual
11. History of Aliens
12. Hollywood Talent Agency Directory
13. Internet Connected World
14. Karate 360
15. Learning Magic

HOLLYWOOD TALENT
AGENCY DIRECTORY

Facebook.com/KambizMostofizadeh

If the Mikazuki Publishing House™ book is not available, place a request with any bookstore to order it for you.

Mikazuki Publishing House™ is a book publisher that started in 2011 in Los Angeles, California. The Mikazuki Publishing House™ . Trademark is protected by the United States Patent Trade Organization, Trademark Registration Number 4323734.